Kehayes playing the guitar 38 North 4th Street in 1932. *hrysanthy Kehayes Grieco*

Chrysanthy with her mother, Iphigenia, and brother, John Kehayes, in their yard at 128 North 6th Street in 1935. *Courtesy of Chrysanthy Kehayes Grieco*

In Branch Brook Park, Yiannoula Juvelis, Maria Vlahakes, and Eleni Chenes, ca. 1932. *Courtesy of the Juvelis Family*

Thomas Louis, the caretaker of St. Demetrios, on New Street enjoying a stroll, ca. 1930s. *Courtesy of the Louis Family*

Helen, Nora, and Margaret Apostolakos in Branch Brook Park, ca. 1938. *Courtesy of Margaret Apostolakos Kostoulakos*

Matina Antonakos Larres with her brother, John, and sister-in-law, ca. 1940s. *Courtesy of Matina Antonakos Larres*

The Mavrode Family is proud to sponsor

"Remembering Newark's Greeks: An American Odyssey"

along with the following groups . . .

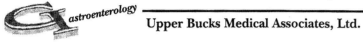

Upper Bucks Medical Associates, Ltd.

John S. Dobrota, M.D.   Frank T. Kucer, M.D.   Ronald P. Markos, M.D.

Upper Bucks Medical Arts Building
817 Lawn Avenue
Sellersville, PA 18960

The Endoscopy Center™

817 Lawn Avenue, Sellersville, PA 18960

Upper Bucks Medical Associates and The Endoscopy Center, John S. Dobrota, M.D., Frank T. Kucer, M.D., Ronald P. Markos, M.D., and Kathleen Lukaszewski, D.O., specializing in the diagnosis and treatment of intestinal diseases, including endoscopy and colonoscopy.

REMEMBERING
NEWARK'S GREEKS:
An American Odyssey
The Newark Public Library Hellenic Heritage Fund

The Hellenic Heritage Fund at The Newark Public Library was created in 2002 and is dedicated to preserving the rich heritage of Greek Americans from Newark and throughout New Jersey.

Remembering Newark's Greeks
An American Odyssey

Angelique Lampros

Introduction by John T. Cunningham

The Donning Company Publishers
184 Business Park Drive, Suite 206
Virginia Beach, VA 23462–6533

Steve Mull, General Manager
Barbara Buchanan, Office Manager
Kathleen Sheridan, Senior Editor
Lynn Parrott, Graphic Designer
Amy Thomann and Mellanie Denny, Imaging Artists
Scott Rule, Director of Marketing
Stephanie Linneman, Marketing Coordinator
Susan Adams, Project Research Coordinator

Mary Taylor, Project Director

Library of Congress Cataloging-in-Publication Data

Lampros, Angelique.
  Remembering Newark's Greeks : an American odyssey / by Angelique Lampros ; introduction by John T. Cunningham.
    p. cm.
  Includes index.
  ISBN–13: 978–1–57864–380–6
  ISBN–10: 1–57864–380–5
  1. Greek Americans—New Jersey—Newark—History. 2. Greek Americans—New Jersey—Newark—Biography. 3. Greek Americans—New Jersey—Newark—Social conditions. 4. Newark (N.J.)—History. 5. Newark (N.J.)—Biography. 6. Newark (N.J.)—Social conditions. 7. Lampros, Angelique—Childhood and youth. I. Title.
  F144.N69G7 2006
  974.9'32004893—dc22
                        2006020655

Published in the United States of America by Walsworth Publishing Company

Photos on p. 55 courtesy of Nick Garbidakis.

Color photos of St. Nicholas Church courtesy of George Diakou unless otherwise noted.

Dedication

Dedicated with respect, gratitude, and love
to the memory of our progenitors,
whose hard work and sacrifices led
to a spectacularly successful odyssey,
which became our legacy.

And to the memory of Charles F. Cummings, mentor,
advocate, and dear friend whose constant
encouragement and interest made possible this book
and the exhibit at the Newark Public Library.

This Newark scene shows Market Street looking west from between Broad and Mulberry Streets in September 1922. Visible on the right are the Newark Theater, bought by Adam A. Adams, Drake College, and Bamberger's, after it expanded to Washington Street.

Courtesy of The Newark Public Library

Contents

Foreword

Greek Life in the Master City

The story of Greek immigration to the United States is a richly endowed human drama of transformation from an old world to a new one. Americans generally envision such a transformation as a historic epoch of Greeks casting their fate far away from the Cradle of Western Civilization. Indeed, when we think of the Greeks, both in the distant and near past, our collective imagination takes us to a grand scale. But, in fact, the immigration of Greek settlers to the United States was a deeply personal journey involving men, women, and children who were heading into an unknown future as anonymous individuals. Their stories are complicated yet accessible to most citizens because of a shared immigrant experience that binds many Americans to their fellow citizens. We are a nation of immigrants, goes the old adage. The Greek American experience is also a poignant and heartening story because it is a part of a larger story of the making of modern America political and cultural democracy. It is a story deserving of a broad understanding by an array of interested citizens, young and old, native born and those recently settled. At a time when the United States and other democratic societies are settling, once again, a tide of new immigrants and facing the challenges wrought by demographic change, the historic settlement of Greeks in America is worthy of deeper consideration. Theirs is an extraordinary narrative of adaptation to a new land, of group and individual progress, and the role of memory in the way history is understood and presented.

Remembering Newark's Greeks: An American Odyssey contributes to our understanding of what has made the United States so appealing to millions of people across the globe since the early years of the Republic. It draws liberally from historical scholarship on the Greek immigrant narrative writ national and local, and it uses testimony from veterans of the past to shed a brilliant light on personal lives and the larger story of a community coming into existence. To be sure, the book also deepens our understanding of one of the nation's most fascinating cities: Newark, New Jersey. Throughout much of its history, the tenor and rhythm of Newark's local culture emerged out of the strenuous efforts by its immigrants and migrants to become new Americans. Newark's immigrants—those forced here by enslavement, those who settled the city because of dire circumstances in their native lands, and those brimming with hope—made Newark into one of the nation's most industrial places; they changed the city's cultural identity and witnessed Newark's rise, decline, and resurgence. In bringing great attention to the Greek American part of the story, this book enriches what we know about that larger immigrant narrative to which Newark is indebted.

The Greek experience in Newark enlivened the city during a period of economic promise and cultural diversity that unfolded from the late nineteenth through the first three decades of the twentieth century. It was the city's Golden Era, the Era of the Master City, 1880–1930. During those years extraordinary changes occurred that moved local life and culture into the modern era. Newark became a major American city, a more diverse and cosmopolitan place with substantial construction in the downtown corridor and reforms in local government. At the time, the city's residents witnessed the ascendancy of the public sphere in education, in the arts and cultural institutions, in recreational spaces, and with greater emphasis on the duties of citizenship. As the reader will soon discover, Greek immigrants and their progeny were hardly bystanders to this emerging change in the way Newarkers entered the then-still-new twentieth century. Over the many years that were to follow, Greek immigrants, arriving from their old lands and their modern Diaspora, established the foundation for a community of remarkable cohesion and purpose. The founding of Greek churches, secular organizations, the business and professional pursuits of its most ambitious sons and daughters, and the nurturing influence of family and friends took place in the face of obstacles endured by all immigrants and newcomers. And not unlike the other immigrants and migrants, the Greeks learned how to navigate Newark's public and private realms. In other words, they learned how to protect and embellish their interests.

The immigrant narrative is the predominant part of Newark's long history as one of the nation's oldest cities. In that sense, for the longest time Newark has been what might be called a diasporic city, a place whose past has been shaped by settlers from Europe, Africa, the American South, the Caribbean, the Pacific Rim, and Asia. With the publication of *Remembering Newark's Greeks*, the story of people changing their lives through immigration, and the story of a city being changed by immigrants on their way to becoming the bedrock of American culture is now brought into sharper focus.

Clement Alexander Price
Board of Governors' Distinguished Service Professor of History
Director, Institute on Ethnicity, Culture, and the Modern Experience
Rutgers University, Newark Campus
Chairman, Save Ellis Island Foundation
May 2006

Acknowledgments

Writing and publishing a book involves the collective effort and shared information of interested and talented individuals. To all the following dedicated individuals, I express a heartfelt appreciation for their valued contributions to this labor of love.

The concept of writing a book about the Greeks of Newark began in 1999 with Peter Markos, who, at that time, asked me to collaborate on this project. Peter and I began our odyssey by gathering materials and collecting stories and photographs from Greek families and friends connected to the early years of Newark. This project led us into a completely new realm of experiences and a variety of people, adding a rewarding dimension to our lives.

The wealth of material and resources we received for this book first culminated in the comprehensive and wonderful exhibit held at the Newark Public Library in October 2002. The success of the exhibit along with our sources, stories, and willingness to see things through set the stage for this book.

My warmest thanks go to Clement Alexander Price, who wrote the informative foreword. His support and continued interest in this project began at a meeting in his office at Rutgers University. He contacted a member of the New Jersey Historical Commission regarding our request for funding to write a book. At that time, he also introduced to Peter and me the late Charles F. Cummings, then the official historian for the City of Newark, who made possible all our accomplishments.

The only way Peter and I can repay our debt to Charles and to his memory is to remember and extol the many attributes of this "gentle man" and gentleman who loved Newark, its history, its architecture and, above all, its people. He willingly imparted his knowledge, becoming our mentor and assisting us through all phases of our endeavors with his constant support and encouragement. We came to value not only his help but also his friendship. Charles made possible, with added support from the wonderful staff at the Newark Public Library, the preservation and inclusion of a permanent Hellenic Heritage Collection in the Charles F. Cummings New Jersey Information Center.

To John T. Cunningham, recognized as "New Jersey's foremost historian," I give my sincerest appreciation for writing the insightful introduction to this book. John, a prolific writer of forty-eight books, two thousand magazine articles, and twenty-five documentary films, focuses his writings on people and his belief that the story of immigration is the foundation of America.

My sincerest thanks go to the staff of the Newark Public Library for their accommodating and welcoming response whenever I needed to collect information and materials for the book, especially Carmelita Bracker, Joe Casale, Heidi Cramer, Sue Mazzeo, Brad Small, Willis Taylor, and Ralph Tohlin.

To all the individuals whose remembrances, documents, and photographs comprise the pages of this book, your parents, grandparents, and relatives would have been proud.

I particularly wish to extol the innumerable talents of three women who graciously and with enthusiasm gladly stepped forward with their respective expertise and knowledge.

First, my gratitude goes to Jeannie Diamandas, a technology training coordinator, for leading me through the labyrinth of technology and devoting countless hours and weekends to the monumental task of acting as project manager. I came to rely on Jeannie and her computer expertise to program each revision of the manuscript and for the preparation of the final format to the specifications of the publisher. Jeannie's invaluable and professional assistance on this project and to me was given freely because, in her words, "It is my heritage, too," and the fact that her family's roots are entwined with the Greeks of Newark. I value her dedicated commitment and friendship.

A million thanks to Marinna Kolaitis, a longtime and close friend with whom I have worked on many other projects throughout the years, for assisting me with the revisions of the narrative. An English professor and author, Marinna, with her love of words, history, and writing, has provided me with a fresh and objective perspective in the final writing of this book. She reminded me that this story reflects "everyone's" story. And she's right. It does seem only fitting that both Marinna and I would collaborate on this book since we both embrace our Greek heritage with love for its history, culture, and traditions.

I was extremely fortunate to have Constance Baboukis, a managing editor, agree to lend her professional expertise to this project. She has been interested in the project ever since the exhibit at the Newark Public Library. During the final stages of the preparation for the book, Connie was invaluable with rewrites, consistency, layouts, and scheduling with the publisher.

Thank you is also extended to Marina Padakis, a senior production editor and the granddaughter of a Greek Newark immigrant, who edited the final drafts of the manuscript with a new and professional editor's eye.

Above all, to my sister, Demi, and my brother, George, thanks for your patience. At times, our home has become an extension of the library housing the collection, a conference room for countless meetings, and the hub of the creative process for putting this book together. I cannot thank you enough for your love and support.

Finally, sincere gratitude to the following sponsors for supporting the publication of this book and for their belief in the merits of this project.

The Mavrode Family of Flemington

Newark Public Library Hellenic Heritage Fund

Upper Bucks Medical Associates, LTD—John S. Dobrota, M.D., Frank T. Kucer, M.D., Ronald P. Markos, M.D.

It has been a delight working closely with the creative professionals Lynn Parrott, Kathy Sheridan, and Mary Taylor at Donning.

I apologize for any inadvertently made errors or omissions.

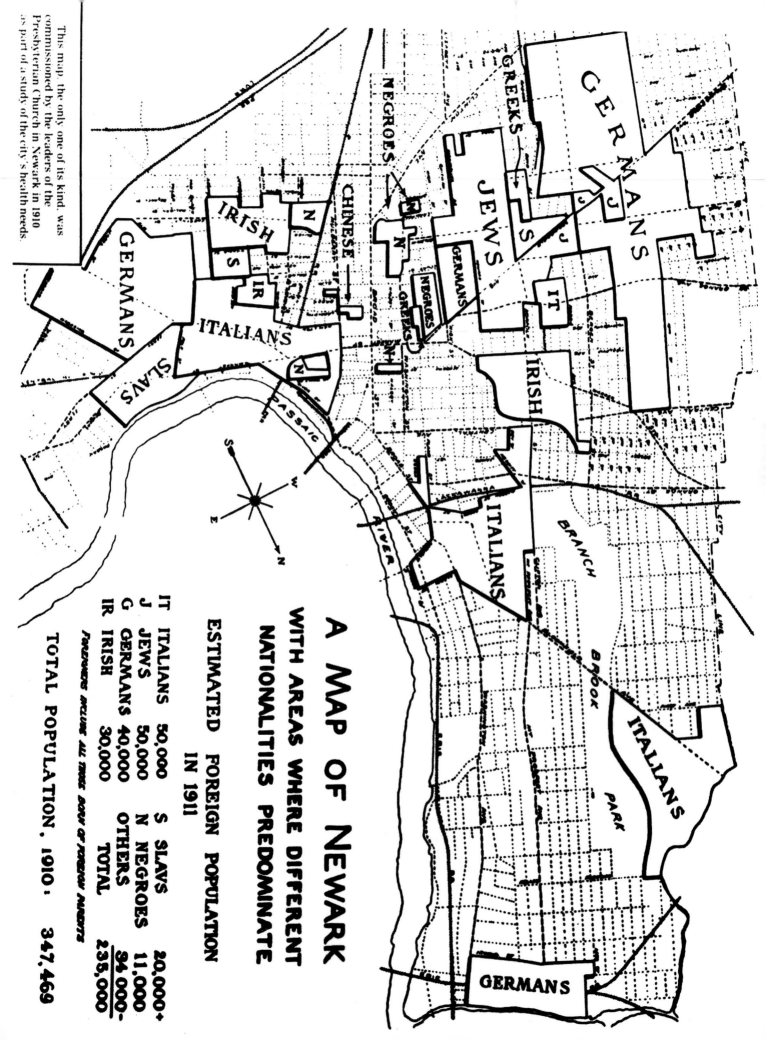

A MAP OF NEWARK

WITH AREAS WHERE DIFFERENT NATIONALITIES PREDOMINATE

ESTIMATED FOREIGN POPULATION IN 1911

IT	ITALIANS	50,000	S SLAVS	20,000+
J	JEWS	50,000	N NEGROES	11,000
G	GERMANS	40,000	OTHERS	94,000
IR	IRISH	30,000	TOTAL	235,000

FOREIGNERS INCLUDE ALL THOSE BORN OF FOREIGN PARENTS

TOTAL POPULATION, 1910: 347,469

This map, the only one of its kind, was commissioned by the leaders of the Presbyterian Church in Newark in 1910 as part of a study of the city's health needs.

Introduction

Newark was a favored place after 1890 for Southern and Eastern European immigrants—Italians, Slavs, Turks, Russian Jews, and Greeks, all of whom found ethnic niches in the growing, prosperous city.

The Greeks were the smallest contingent of Newark's immigrants; a 1910 map of Newark's foreign populations showed fewer than 10,000 Greeks in a city with a population of 347,469. Their influence on Newark, however, far superseded their relatively small numbers.

The map showed two "Greek areas" in the city, both squeezed among the Germans—Italians, Jews, Slavs, Blacks, and others who had earlier ventured into a vital city that offered a first giant step into America.

That map, church records, and bits of meager information in Newark Library files offered the only major evidence of the Greek population in the city during most of the early twentieth century. That is what makes this book so important. Its co-curators have found those who remember the earliest days of Greeks in Newark, have recorded their stories, and the author has assembled those recollections and pictures here in a fascinating document.

Without this arduous and loving effort, the colorful saga of the city's Hellenic people, their customs, churches, solidarity, and immigrant base might be nothing but footnotes in broader histories of Newark.

By 1890 powerful forces in Greece made migration to America both necessary and desirable. The raisin and currant crops, so necessary to many winemakers outside Greece, failed. The yoke of the Ottoman Empire prevailed in portions of the nation. Poverty was rife. Those conditions, combined with glowing accounts sent back by Greeks who already lived in America, fueled the desire to see the New World.

Greeks left their sun-baked seaside villages and homes in the mountains, generally walking long distances to ports to board immigrant vessels. They endured long voyages in steerage, often lasting three weeks, through the calm Mediterranean Sea and across the turbulent Atlantic Ocean to New York Harbor.

Ellis Island, while frightening in prospect, presented little difficulty, and the Greeks, along with many other nationalities, streamed from the island to seek work in their new country. Although most of them had lived on farms or on sparsely settled mountain slopes, they were forced to turn to nearby cities for their futures. Newark, only a short train ride from Hoboken and Jersey City, proved to be one of the most enticing.

The earliest Newark Greeks worked in small food dispensaries or shined shoes in railroad stations and along city streets. The earliest food workers opened their own restaurants and became well known for Greek cooking. The Greek shoeshine boys, however, were mistreated, overworked, and cheated out of their earnings by fellow Greeks who owned the shoeshine parlors.

Eventually, many Greek men found work in Newark's leather factories. One of those employers, the Solomon Tannery, employed 150 to 200 Greek immigrants by 1908. Scores of Greek women rolled and packed "smokes" (mostly cigars).

The most compelling work by Greek immigrants was in the Thomas Edison Laboratories in nearby West Orange. Spiros Givas, shop foreman at Edison from 1906 to 1916, was said to have hired "many, many Greeks."

These pioneer Greeks, mostly young men, saved earnestly either to return home to live or, more likely, to marry childhood sweethearts and bring them to America.

After work, the young men gathered at one of the city's *kafeneia* (coffeehouses) to exchange hopes, dreams, memories, and job prospects. In time, within organized societies, they reached out to offer assistance and social support to newly arrived Greeks.

The main stabilizing force in this wave of immigration was the Greek Orthodox Church. The first wooden church was erected on Academy Street in front of the Morris Canal. The present St. Nicholas Church on High Street was dedicated on December 18, 1924.

With their spiritual center in place and Greeks in positions of community leadership, those who had experienced the modern Odyssey from Greece to Ellis Island to Newark became a solid part of their chosen community.

This is their story, often in their own words and most certainly in their own pictures. It rescues the Greek heritage of the city from possible oblivion in a sea of indifference. Most important, it adds a colorful dimension to the persevering, imaginative, diversified people who have combined to create a major city.

John T. Cunningham
Florham Park, New Jersey
April 27, 2006

1

$\mathcal{L}$eaving the "cradle of Western Civilization and the birthplace of democracy" to travel to an unknown land with "streets paved in gold," the Greeks began their odyssey to America. They ventured forth from the villages of Peloponnesos to the mountains of Thessaly, from the islands of the Aegean and Ionian Seas to Asia Minor, embarking on a journey of hope. Though most came from Greece proper and its islands, many traveled a circuitous route from Turkey, Egypt, Syria, Bulgaria, Romania, Albania, Hungary, Russia, or Austria. The young Greek men— for it was mostly men at that time—came with the hope of finding work to support their families left behind, to make their fortune and return someday to their homes in Greece a financial success.

The Greeks came because of lack of work and crushing poverty in their beautiful homeland. Like Odysseus in their legends, the Greeks roamed the world.

⌐John Cunningham[1]

Map of Greece
Courtesy of New Oxford American Dictionary © 2005 by Oxford University Press, Inc. Used with permission.

The Tholos of Marmaria is the sanctuary of the goddess Athena, at Delphi on Mount Parnassus.

The town and port of Gytheion in Peloponnesos, viewed from the connected Island of Cranae, was a main port until the Isthmus of Corinth was built.

My grandfather was born in Politsi in Peloponnesos. The views from his village were equally stunning as the depth of poverty of the region. When asked what was his hometown's best attributes, he would reply, "petres" (rocks).
　Paul (Papandreopoulos) Andrews

The late nineteenth and early twentieth centuries saw a major exodus from the peninsula of Peloponnesos, the southern part of mainland Greece, due to a devastating drought. *Horia* (villages) scattered throughout this area depended primarily on their crops of currants, most of which were exported to France's international wineries. The decimation of their principal export crop caused prices to fall and trade to decline. Furthermore, farmers had no alternative means of farming or employment, resulting in impoverishment and loss of income. Eventually, throughout the mainland and islands of Greece, poverty became the primary cause of departure.

The Mani was a bleak, barren, forbidding mountainous region, devoid of fertile land. They left from the port of Gytheion to go to Piraeus and from there to America.
　John Koronakos

My father-in-law was born in the wild mountains of Peloponnesos in Greece, an extremely poor area. When the chief product of the region, the raisin crop, failed, many young men, he among them, emigrated to the New World in 1902. My father-in-law's village was close to the Mani, and he was called a Maniati.
　Anastasia G. Bravakis

To provide support for family and the culturally necessary dowries for daughters and sisters, men left their homeland.

Gus Gevas, who was born in Tritea, within eyesight of Delphi, was one of the three sons and two daughters of a poor cobbler family. He went to school for two years in his village, then at the age of eight he went to a larger neighboring village to work in a grocery store. Finally, he left Greece at the age of thirteen to come to America in order to earn dowries for his sisters.
 ⌒ James Gevas

Fathers who were already here and working sent for children, wives, brothers, sisters, and even fellow villagers. Women and children, when they eventually emigrated, came to join husbands, fathers, brothers, or other relatives either to work with them or care for the homes.

We went to my mother's two brothers, who lived in Newark. My aunt had two babies, and I stayed with her to take care of them because I was too young to work. My sister, at sixteen, went to work in a steel mill. They made the worst mistake in not sending us to school. They felt it was not important for us to be educated.
 ⌒ Jennie Moutis

Mother came to make money to go back to Greece and get married. She was ten years old and came with her sister and father. Her uncle lied to Immigration, saying he would send her to school; he never did. Although she was young, grandfather wanted her to work, but they would not hire her because she was too young. He wouldn't let her go to school. She had a tremendous desire to learn, so she kept after us as we were growing up, pushing us to continue our education.
 ⌒ Spiro Poulos

Others left their villages and towns to support the parents left behind, thinking they would have better opportunities for meaningful employment.

Mary Diakoumakou, my grandmother, left Greece in August of 1910. She wanted to make money and return to help her family realize a better life. Her family were farmers, poor but proud. In her family's home she had food and shelter. Although an exceptional student and an elementary school graduate, there was little opportunity for a good position in the village for a woman. Her father was sick, and the family had fallen on hard times. She was fifteen years old when she decided to leave. Her parents did not want her to go, but she was determined. Everyone was sad, and the whole village came out to say goodbye and wish her good luck. She never was able to go back to Greece, and this was

Constantine Nickolopoulos, in Greek village attire, takes a final photograph with his son, Themistocles, who will soon leave the village of Politsi and travel to America, eventually settling in Newark, ca. the 1890s.
Courtesy of Paul (Papandreopoulos) Andrews

the last time she was to see her parents, her brother, and two of her three sisters (her one sister came to America several years later). Mary came on the steamer Martha Washington. On the voyage over, she was very homesick and often cried. At times, she also felt very seasick. The passage over cost 34 dollars. For that she had her own little cabin, but had to eat in a public dining room. She entered the United States at Ellis Island. Her cousin was waiting to meet her there and was able to help her get through immigration on the first day. She went to live with him and some other cousins first in New York and then they moved to Newark.

◦⁓ Barbara Christos Massad

Some came to these shores to get married, since in America there was no need for a dowry.

My parents came from the island of Mytilene (Lesbos) for opportunity and freedom. My mother was one of five girls, and my grandfather avoided dowries by bringing them to America to find husbands.

◦⁓ Bessie Kostins Mamalou

Still others left their homeland because parts of Greece were still under the yoke of the Ottoman Empire. After the demise of the Byzantine Empire with the fall of Constantinople in 1453, Greece was intermittently under Ottoman occupation until the outbreak of the Greek War of Independence in 1821. In 1829, with the help of Russia, Great Britain, and France, a peace treaty allowed Greek self-rule. At the time, with Athens as its capital, Greece consisted only of the region south of Thermopylae plus the island of Euboea.

My parents came to America because the island of Samos was under the control of the Ottoman Empire.

◦⁓ James Petine

They came from the island of Mytilene to escape Turkish rule.

◦⁓ Peter Jovanis

Gradually, after the Balkan Wars, Greece regained Thessaly and part of Epirus in 1881, Crete in 1908, and in 1913, prior to World War I, the remaining parts of Epirus and Macedonia, as well as most of the Aegean Islands.

When World War I began in Europe in August 1914, Greece, with the support of Eleutherios Venizelos, the prime minister, joined the Allies. The Allies won in 1918, and Greece gained most of the west Thrace shore of the Aegean Sea. The twelve Dodecanese Islands voted for union with Greece.[2]

I came to America when I was about nine years old. My father sent money for my passage. The war was on and we went from Patmos to Italy, stayed there

a month, then to Gibraltar and remained there for two weeks because of the fear of German submarines. Finally, we left in a twenty-ship convoy that took twenty days to arrive in Boston, Massachusetts, on August 16, 1917.
⌒ Tom Manos

One of the great catastrophic events that effected a major deportation of Greece's inhabitants took place in Asia Minor—the burning of Smyrna in 1922. This ancient city, now Izmir, was once believed to be the birthplace of Homer, and a temple was even erected in honor of the poet. Located on the western peninsula of Asia, also known as Anatolia, this legendary city was occupied by Turkey after World War I, when Kemal Attaturk's insurgent troops entered the city. The majority of people living at that time in Asia Minor were Greek and tended to be more highly skilled and professionally educated.

It was clear Iphigenia's life was changed forever when in 1918, Attaturk's troops came to that town and ordered all boys and men from the ages of fourteen to forty-five to be rounded up. They were to comprise the army that was to be taken to the interior of Turkey, to Balukiser. They were to do battle against their fellows who came from Greece to help their brethren in the struggle against the Ottoman Empire. In this group was Reverend Panayoti Mamouni, Iphigenia's father, who refused to fight and was consequently martyred and declared a saint of the church for his heroism in bringing the Sacrament to his fellow men, some as they were injured and others as they lay dying.
⌒ Chrysanthy Kehayes Grieco

Others who came to America returned to their home-land with their savings and with the intention of starting a new life with their families.

My father, Straty Buclary, came to the United States in 1898 aboard the steamer transport Sherman, *working as a fireman in the boiler room. He left the ship in San Francisco, worked in lumber camps for the Bremerton Navy Yard, bought a fishing boat, and became a commercial fisherman. He learned English in the process and became an American citizen in 1905. At the end of World War I, he returned to Ivaley, Turkey, to take over the family export business and to marry. On August 27, 1922, the Turks invaded Ivaley*

The four Polychronopoulos sisters are pictured from left: Mrs. Coniaris, Mrs. Poulos, Mrs. Spanioles, and Mrs. Beretsos, ca. 1917.
Courtesy of the Coniaris Family

and began to massacre the inhabitants. He instructed his mother to sew an American flag and display it in the window of their home. The Turks respected the flag and did not harm them. The United States ordered all American citizens to leave the country. Fearing for their lives, the family left on the King Alexander and docked in New York on January 8, 1923.

  Apolon Buclary

The émigrés ventured forth from the ports of Greece and the western coast of Asia Minor seeking work in America. The trip to America from Greece was arduous, taking as little as twenty days but sometimes months. Reaching the ships also involved hardships—walking miles and days from the villages to reach the various ports in Piraeus and Patras. Most traveled in steerage and landed at Ellis Island. Among the ships that brought them were the *Acropolis*, *Athinai*, *Byron*, *Constantinople* (*King Alexander*), *Edison*, and *Patris*.

Gus Janulis remembers when he was fourteen years old and traveled to America.

> *I came to America on a beautiful day in August of 1923. We were taken into Ellis Island, and as we entered the huge building, several women were there to welcome us. They gave us a glass of milk and a few Social Tea biscuits. After we finished them, we were given a bar of soap and a big towel to take a shower. We stayed there several days. The food was delicious, much different from our meals in Greece. I was waiting and waiting and I thought my brother Theodore had forgotten about me. Then one day he came and we both went before a judge who asked my brother, "What are you going to do with this fat boy?" He said, "I have a delicatessen store," and the judge told him that he must place me in school for two years before he could use me in his store. So he did just that. He gave me a nice white apron the next day and put me to work. God bless him.*
>
>   Gus Janulis

Arriving on the *Byron* in 1920, Jennie Moutis, age thirteen, came with her sixteen-year-old sister and father. Her experience upon landing at Ellis Island was quite different.

> *My father had running eyes, and they took him upstairs to the hospital. We did not see him for two days. We slept on chairs, there was such poverty on Ellis Island. They gave us tea and paximadia (biscuits) for two days.*
>
>   Jennie Moutis

This photograph taken in the village of Arona in Macedonia shows Eleni Lambrou Katsara holding her son, Nicholas, with her daughter, Anoula, on her left and her son, Demetrios, on her right, July 19, 1932.
Courtesy of the Lampros Family

Nicholas Lampros, who departed his home in the village of Moschopatomo in 1909 when it was under Turkish occupation, was forced to leave his sister, Eleni Lambrou. They reunited when he visited Greece after a sixty-year separation.

The passenger ship *Byron* journeys from Greece to the United States. It made its last voyage in 1935 when it returned to Greece and was placed in dry dock.
Courtesy of Steamship Historical Society of America

This is the steamship ticket of Chris and Anna Sarandoulias for travel on the *Byron* from Greece to America, 1934.
Courtesy of the Sarandoulias Family

My grandfather, John Economou, was a steamship ticket agent who helped locate jobs for dozens of Greek immigrants.
DOT DENICHOLAS BISBAS

The Statue of Liberty was the first sign of welcome to the new country as ships entered the New York Harbor.
Courtesy of Marinna Kolaitis

Documents necessary for entry to the United States included passports, visas, and declarations of intent, or affidavits of support. Upon arrival, the immigrants prepared certificates of arrival and petitions for naturalization. During this same period, many men worked on ships sailing to distant ports. Some without documents took the opportunity to jump ship in America.

My father worked as a chef on a ship, and I would see him every four or five years. In 1936, I left the island of Andros and went with him on the ship. When we came to the United States, he thought it would be best for me to stay because of the war in Europe. He wanted me to have a better life. I jumped ship at the age of eighteen. I never saw my father again.
George Mendrinos

Some families, having settled in the United States prior to World War I, decided to return to Greece, taking their American-born children with them. Others sent their children back to their homeland to visit with relatives for a while. These decisions caused unanticipated consequences for the children. Global conditions and family situations disrupted well-intentioned plans. As a result, families only intending to visit ended up staying for years because of events beyond their control.

I was taken to Sparta to live with my aunt so my grandfather would get to know me. My parents were going to take a trip to visit and bring me back. I was two and remained in Greece because World War I broke out, then my father died. It was not until I was sixteen when I finally received a ticket on the Byron *to return to a land and family I did not really know.*
Mary Vasiliow Pantelis

After his family's fortune sharply declined, my grandfather came to America. My grandmother died of an infection caused by a piece of wood that lodged against her abdomen while she was chopping wood. They had a four-year-old daughter, born in the U.S., Olga Linardakis. Grandfather had done well, but decided that he did not want his children brought up in America, so he took them back to Greece. He remarried, and his new wife did not want to raise his daughter, Olga. She was given to the family of Captain Sachariou to raise

Returning to America at the age of sixteen after living in Greece, Mary Vasiliow kept this menu from the *Byron*. An inscription in Greek, translates to "O Byron, the ship that brought me to this black, foreign land in 1927."
Courtesy of Mary Vasiliow Pantelis

and effectively was a beloved maid to the family. The children of Captain Sachariou went to college, but she only went to school for one year. The stepmother and grandfather raised her brother, Nick. He worked as a helper to a chimney maker. Olga finally went back to the U.S. and initially stayed with the Gus Linardakis family in Newark for a short while. One of the Gevas family members introduced her to her future husband, Gus Gevas.
    James Gevas

Once settled, Greeks wanted the type of family structure, life, and community they had in Greece. Some brought their wives and children to Newark, while others sent for a bride or traveled to Greece and returned with one.

Mother and Father were neighbors in Bouharina, Kozane, and after establishing a business in Newark, he went back to marry the neighbor's daughter. They came to America to have a richer life and for the land opportunity.
    Helen Peters Cap

Smaller than New York City, Newark had a rural environment, which made it more attractive to immigrants seeking work and a place to live. Its connecting rivers and canals gave rise to various industries that provided opportunities for work in the leather tanning and cigar factories, breweries, and the nearby Thomas Edison Laboratory in West Orange.

One of the first jobs available to them was as shoeshine boys, or bootblacks, working for already established immigrants in the business. They worked sixteen hours a day, seven days a week, living together in quarters provided by the owner. As with many immigrants, those who came before them exploited many.

My father came as a young boy in 1896 from Tripoli and began by shining shoes in a shoeshine parlor. At night, all the boys slept in the back room. My father slept under the sink. There was no heat, the water dripped on his head, and it was freezing. He vowed he would never be poor like that again.
    Dorothea Adams Pantages

As they learned the trade, they gradually opened their own shoeshine, hat cleaning and blocking, and shoe repair businesses near busy intersections and city offices.

Others found jobs as laborers in leather tanning and cigar factories. One leather factory, the Soloman Tannery on Nesbit and Sussex Avenues, employed 150 to 200 Greek immigrants by 1908. The principal place of employment for women was in the cigar factories in Newark, where they rolled and packed "smokes."[3]

George Petropoulos and his wife, Victoria, arrive in New York after their marriage in Greece to settle in Newark, ca. 1929.
Courtesy of Helen Peters Cap

Documents

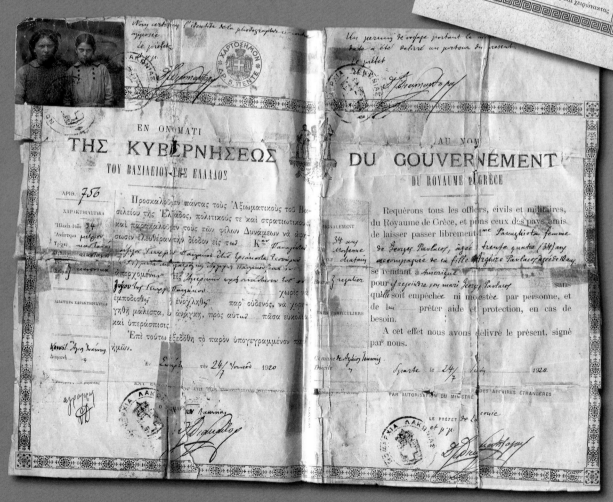

A temporary Greek passport ca. 1921 was issued by the Greek Consulate in New York to Elene Sfalanga in order for her to travel to Greece.
Courtesy of Peter Mehalaris

This Greek passport and American visa from the American Consulate in Athens, Greece, was issued to Panagiota Pavlakos and her daughter, Anna, age thirteen, to enter Ellis Island, New York, June 26, 1920.
Courtesy of the Sam Markos Family

This application for a Certificate of Arrival and Preliminary Form for Petition for Naturalization was prepared by Sylvia Pappas to join her two brothers and a sister living in Newark, New Jersey, in September 1914.
Courtesy of Ileana N. Saros

The United States of America Declaration of Intention of John Bravakis to become a citizen, pledging allegiance to the United States of America, January 24, 1922.
Courtesy of Theodore J. Bravakis

My grandfather started as a laborer in a leather factory and later he got into pushcarts. My father, on the other hand, was in the tailor business. At first, he worked in the shoe repair business with George Argyris, who took all immigrants. Mother got a job at the Wait and Barnes Cigar Factory on Wicker Street from 1922 through 1927, when the factory moved.

 Reverend Peter Kostakos

My grandmother worked for the Lewis Cigar Factory rolling cigars for forty years until it went out of business. The first week she received no pay because she was just learning how to do it. After that, she received three dollars a week for working ten hours a day all week and five hours on Saturdays. Because she worked hard and was good at the technique of rolling cigars, she was able to increase her pay to seven dollars a week and then more. This was not an easy job. Many days she would get sick from the smell of the cigars.

 Barbara Christos Massad

George Pavlakos stands in front of his fruit and vegetable market at 125 Mulberry Street, Newark, ca. 1924.
Courtesy of the Pavlakos Family

Marina Motsovolos Corodemus started working at Lou's Cigar Factory rolling cigars. She enjoyed working there since there were many Greek workers.
ᛣᚱ Helen Corodemus Loukedis

This December 10, 1914, photo shows the Edison Industrial buildings complex in West Orange, where many Greek immigrants from Newark worked.
Courtesy of The Newark Public Library

Still others got into the food business, starting as dishwashers and becoming countermen and waiters; others opened up fruit stands or sold produce on pushcarts.

My grandfather, George Pavlakos, had a fruit stand on Market Street and Mulberry Street near Penn Station. My mother worked in a toothpaste factory in Newark.
ᛣᚱ Antoinette Markos Genakos

My father was an iceman. He easily hoisted one hundred-pound blocks of ice on his shoulder and carried them to the large commercial iceboxes in the restaurants he served. After my father's death, Mother would make wine to sell at the kafeneia *(coffeehouses). My brother, George, would go down with one gallon of wine, I'd go down later with another gallon, collect the money, and bring it back to Mother, who always worried about being caught. . . . Neighbors and our Italian landlord protected her from the police because she was a widow raising her children alone. She never let us take anything from anyone.*
ᛣᚱ Theodore J. Bravakis

William Zois and his staff in front of the shop advertising a donation to the Mississippi Flood victims, ca. 1912.
Courtesy of Leon Zois and family

My father, Dionisios Papanastasio Skopelitis (Dan Skopas), helped the island of Lemnos have electricity and water in their homes. At the hospital in Lemnos there is a plaque commemorating his hard work to obtain ambulances for the hospital.
ANGELIKI MORRIS ANDERSON

My dad worked in restaurants as a short-order cook. In the early years, my mother did embroidery on babywear at home. As a child during the summer months, I helped her.
〜 Angelina Halamandaris Aretakis

A number of immigrant groups, including the Greeks, ventured outside of the city to seek work at the Thomas Edison Laboratories in West Orange.

My father, Spyros A. Givas, was shop foreman at the Edison Company from 1906 to 1916. My father told me he hired many, many Greeks while he was there.
〜 Loula Givas Georges

Men and women tried everything to support themselves and the families they brought to America. Greeks who came from the northern regions of Greece and were active in the fur business utilized this expertise at various fur establishments that opened in Newark and New York.

My mother was raising four children. She couldn't speak the language very well, but she had a friend in New York who got her a job putting linings in mink coats as a finisher. This was a seasonal job for six or seven months. There was no welfare, but this carried the family the other three months. Mother would get up at 6 a.m., leave soon after that, and she would return at 8 p.m. We only saw her on weekends. My sister took care of the children.
〜 Michael Paskas

To help newly arrived immigrants, the formation of *koinotita* (community) began within the already established enclaves of Germans, Irish, Italians, Blacks, and Jews, as shown in the 1910 map of Newark. Gradually the Greeks working together roomed together, beginning to meet socially in one of the first gathering places for the Greek male community, the *kafeneion* (coffee house). Here young Greek men could meet, play cards, drink, talk about home, and discuss Greek politics.

In my time and my neighborhood, we had some special coffeehouses. Barba Yiannis, originally from the island of Samos, owned one of those. Barba Yiannis was in his 80s. In his kafeneion *(coffeehouse), he served great appetizers, and whiskey in coffee cups. Sometimes some of the old men would bring in their instruments, and we would go through the night drinking and singing Greek folk songs. What a wonderful education for a young man like me, learning*

both the traditions and songs of Greece. Others also owned
*kafeneia (coffeehouses) on the same street. They included Tsanras,
[owned by] George Spiropoulos and Stathis Georgatsos.*
⌒ Reverend George A. Xenofanes

Teenagers growing up usually had to work at menial jobs while going to
school in order to supplement their family's income. They delivered Greek
and American newspapers after school, worked in the Greek bakeries,
restaurants, floral shops, and theaters, and delivered milk, ice, coal, and
produce to customers.

> *My father was a waiter at the Douglas Hotel, and Mom took
> care of children. When I was about eight years old, I worked for
> Tachinos grocery store at the corner of Warren and Summit Streets
> after school. I would walk on the other side of the street so I didn't
> have to go to work, but Mr. Tachinos would be waiting outside
> and say, "Go change your clothes and come to work."*
> ⌒ Gus Genakos

The first émigrés came either alone or with compatriots. Unable to
speak the language, living from hand to mouth in a foreign environment
with no real family, they gravitated toward small enclaves consisting
of members of the same village, town, and area from which they came.
Originally, small ethnic societies formed to help those they had left
behind. Gradually they began to offer assistance and social support to
the newly arrived emigrants.

> *Parnassus Society was the first ethnic organization to have a society
> incorporated in the United States. It was formed by Newark
> Greeks who came from the village of Tretea, located at the base of
> Mount Parnassus.*
> ⌒ James Gevas

These early pioneers from Greece worked hard, supported their families in
their homeland, and began to establish a life and a community here. They
realized they would remain in America and, specifically, metropolitan
Newark. Now life with family and friends, and the building of a
permanent community began in earnest and flourished.

Adam A. Adams built a school and playground in
Tegea, Tripolis, ca. 1935.
Courtesy of the Adams and Pantages Family

*Anthony and Anastasia Javas
brought water to all the homes
of the village Dirachion in the
Peloponnesos and built a school for
the children. The Javas brothers
were also generous contributors to St.
Nicholas Greek Orthodox Church.*
HELEN ANGELIDES

At their engagement in Athens, Greece, standing from left are: Irene Grammata and Michael Costopoulos, with sister Kettie Grammata; seated are George (father), Argyro, and Persephone (mother) Grammata in June 1925.
Courtesy of Angelique Costopoulos Gionis

Michael Costopoulos was a naturalized American citizen. After his four sisters were married, he sold his restaurant and took a trip to Greece to marry. His cousins, who were close friends of the family, introduced him to Irene Grammata.

MARY VASILIOW PANTELIS

After her marriage and prior to her departure for Newark, Irene Grammata wrote an entry in the diary of her sister, Kettie, expressing her trepidation at leaving her family, ca. the 1920s.
Courtesy of Catherine N. Yatrakis

My little sister,

Here we are on the eve of our separation and how lucky I am to have found a blank page in your memory book to leave you with a few words of wisdom, or rather, I should say sisterly advice, and a few promises, too. As the time for my departure to America draws near, I am filled with nostalgia, love, and concern for our parents, our home, and most of all for you my little sister, Kettie. Continue to be strong, to love and appreciate our dear parents. I know you too will find the happiness and love I have found. Mere words cannot convey or express my feelings today, my little sister. I want to tell you how much I love you and assure you that the distance and miles will never really separate us. Nothing can change the way we feel for one another and for our family. I will forever be grateful for you staying close to our parents. I leave you with my love and good wishes.

Nina [Irene] Costopoulos, December 30, 1925

TRANSLATION COURTESY OF MARIA D. YATRAKIS

In the last family photograph together, Vassiliki and Demetrios Kiriakarakos stand on either side of their Uncle George and Aunt Katherine Kyriakarakos and their young cousins, ca. 1935.
Courtesy of the Lampros Family

Letter from Nicholas Lampros to his future brother-in-law in Gytheion dated January 25, 1935, on his business letterhead.
Courtesy of the Lampros Family

January 25, 1935

My dear brother Mitso,

I received your letter with great happiness and I believe that very quickly we will see each other again. I believe you will be here about March because for Vassiliki and me time passes very slowly until we meet. I hope my letter finds you both in good health. I see our uncles often here and they are all fine and awaiting your arrival. Mitso, we have had a very heavy winter with a great deal of snow and I am preparing for Easter to finish my work so that I will be free when Vassiliki arrives and I can show her around.

I kiss you, your brother Nikos

Mother, age four, and her brothers, Nicholas, twelve, and Demetrios, ten, born in Lewiston, Maine, journeyed with their parents to Gytheion, Greece, for a visit. The advent of World War I affected their lives. Our grandmother was pregnant and died in childbirth, and our grandfather died a year later of pneumonia while serving in the Greek army. Orphaned, the children were raised by their father's brother, George. After the older brother, Nicholas, died of a high fever, Demetrios went to Athens to live with his aunt, where he eventually attended the Maritime College of Athens, receiving his certificate of chief engineer. Mother remained in Gytheion with her uncle's family, attending elementary school. Demetrios, assigned to the Byron, *made many trips to American ports. On these trips, he visited family living in Newark and met Nicholas Lampros. He decided Nick would become Mother's husband. In the spring of 1935, Mother returned to the land of her birth, escorted by her brother on the* Byron's *last voyage, for her wedding.*

DEMETRA LAMPROS

Probably the most influencing force in our lives was the church. We were raised with such a strong sense of faith and devotion; through the hard times and good times, the church was our beacon.

Stella Visas Economo

2

Establishing Churches

*T*he Greek Orthodox parishes in America "were founded by the faith, dedication and initiative of the lay immigrants who recognized the need for a parish mission to meet their religious and sacramental needs."[4] Equally important, they felt that a church community would perpetuate the Greek language and the traditions of the homeland.

> *Monasteries in Greece maintained the languages, and the religion, the historical basis of the Greek Orthodox Church.*
> ⌐ Reverend James A. Aloupis

The center of the Greek Orthodox Church is the Divine Liturgy, dating back to Byzantium. The service traditionally includes the reading of the Holy Scriptures and the faithful partaking in Holy Communion. The liturgy is chanted by the priest with the *psalti* (chanter) providing the responses. Holy icons are a significant part of the Eastern Orthodox religion. Paintings of Christ, the *Panayia Theotokou* (the Mother of God), and the Saints are strategically placed throughout the church as well as in the homes of the faithful. For the Greek immigrant family arriving in Newark, the church became a home away from home, preserving the Eastern Orthodox faith, the language of their forefathers, and the traditions of their mother country.

Postcard showing the Monastery of St. Prodromos, which is located in Seres, Macedonia, in northern Greece.

Standing on the front steps of the newly built St. Nicholas Greek Orthodox Church on Academy Street, ca. 1920, are priests and parishioners including, in front row, fourth from the left, Eleftherios Kiriakou Venizelos, prime minister of Greece.
Courtesy of the Adams and Pantages families

St. Nicholas Church, the Mother Church of New Jersey

In the first decade of the twentieth century, a handful of Greek male immigrants living in Newark and the surrounding areas established the first Greek Orthodox church in New Jersey. As the leaders of the church, these men helped to make the church a reality by finding and purchasing property, building the church, and hiring a priest. Reverend Adamakos, the first pastor of this small community, held services on the second floor of a building located on Washington Street and Market Street near the new Bamberger's department store. Eventually, this group became the administrative head of the church, the *Symboulion*, or Board of Trustees, who made the final decisions for the church.

With a growing congregation, in 1906 the church was incorporated as St. Nicholas Greek Orthodox Church of the City of Newark. Worship services were held at Lyric Hall, 303 Plane Street. The Very Reverend Prousianos assumed the pastoral obligations of this burgeoning religious community in 1907. That same year, at an informal meeting of church members, the group resolved to collect funds toward the eventual purchase of land located at 149 Academy Street in front of the Morris Canal, a major commerce route that once flowed across the state of New Jersey. At an approximate cost of $9,000, the building of the first Greek Orthodox church in Newark was completed in 1909.

> *St. Nicholas was a wooden building with one great big room having no icons except for an altar screen. Greek School, funerals, weddings, meetings, and festivities all took place in that room. The Morris Canal ran behind the church. Kids in Greek school would play in the [now dry] canal after school.*
> — Joanna Gellas

Prior to World War I, events in Greece had a direct effect on the Greek Orthodox church in America. Two political factions existed at that time: the Royalists, who were loyal to King Constantine, wanted Greece to remain neutral in the war, and the Venizelists, loyal to Prime Minister Eleftherios Venizelos, wanted Greece to side with the Allies. During this period of unrest in Greece, the faithful took political sides, which hampered the church's progress.[5] In Greece, church and state issues were not separate; likewise, this concept of dual church and state control carried over to the parishioners of St. Nicholas, who became wholly involved in the political events of Greece.

> *My father was more concerned with the politics of Greece than America, as were most of his acquaintances, and many heated arguments ensued between friends: Royalists against Venizelists. My father was a Venizelist.*
> — Theodore J. Bravakis

Although officially under the jurisdiction of both the Patriarchate of Constantinople and the Holy Synod Church of Greece, the Greek Orthodox churches in America functioned for the most part autonomously. Lay leaders of each church were able to appoint or dismiss their priests, a practice similar to the Protestant hierarchy in

The corner of Market and Beaver Streets in 1916. In 1906, Lyric Hall, on the right, housed St. Nicholas Greek Orthodox Church on the second floor.
Courtesy of The Newark Public Library

Reverend Thomas Papageorgiou was pastor of St. Nicholas Greek Orthodox Church on Academy Street 1912–17, ca. 1921.
Courtesy of Calomira Papageorge Canaris

America. During this volatile time, Reverend Thomas Papageorgiou was St. Nicholas's officiating priest. However, another political faction of the Newark community wished to appoint Reverend Vasileos Daskalakis, whose political persuasion concurred with theirs. This political harangue within the church community soon became an issue across the ocean. As political power changed hands in Greece, so did the hierarchy of the Holy Synod of Greece, who now interfered with the appointment or dismissal of priests in America.

Letters were sent back and forth from Newark to Greece, with a reply from Archbishop Theoklitos, at that time head of the Holy Synod of Greece:

From Kingdom of Greece, the Holy Synod of the Church of Greece

To the Ecclesiastical Council of the Greek Orthodox Community of Newark, New Jersey

In answer to your letters of June 17th through the 30th informing you of the Synod's decision that we had informed you for 22nd April that the only acceptable priest is the Reverend Thomas Papageorgiou to whom you owe respect and the required support. In addition, we inform you [that] the non-conformist Reverend Vasileos Daskalakis is forbidden to perform any priestly duties and that he was called upon to defend himself in front of the Holy Synod.[6]

Ultimately, the matter was settled with the appointment of Reverend George Spyridakis in December 1918. Reverend Spyridakis was born in Crete and was graduated from Holy Cross Seminary, Jerusalem. His spiritual duties included serving all his parishioners residing in Essex, Union, Passaic, Hudson, and Monmouth Counties. During those early days, he faced many hardships, having to travel by public transportation to perform weddings, funerals, and baptisms, or to visit patients in the various hospitals throughout the different towns.

I was awed by Father Spyridakis; his strengths were monumental. He was very bright and highly educated. Father Spyridakis was a genuine hero.
⌒ James Gevas

Father Spyridakis also realized the importance of the younger generation if the Greek Orthodox church in America were to survive; therefore, he initiated Greek afternoon and Sunday School programs that took place in the church hall with him and his wife, Presbytera Theodoroula Spyridakis, at the helm.

In those days, Greek school was from 4 to 6 p.m., five days a week. In the fall the boys would rebel against Greek school by continuing to play football in the lot near the church beyond 4 o'clock.
⌒ John Antonakos

Energetic and dedicated, Reverend Spyridakis was building a congregation, with church attendance increasing to the point where the services of the major religious holidays, particularly the Easter services of Holy Week, needed the use of St. Paul's Episcopal Church on High and West Market Streets.

> *Church was the core of the Greek community, and St. Nicholas, the church that we attended, had the largest congregation in Newark.*
> ⌒ Helen Galanoplos

The need for a new, larger church became evident, and a fundraising campaign began in 1919, enabling the community to receive a loan from the Broad and Market National Bank of Newark for $50,000, with Charles F. Ackerman selected as the architect. At that time, the Becker Construction Company was contracted to build the existing structure on High Street in Newark. The building was completed, and a *thyranoixia* (opening of the doors) and dedication were held on Sunday, December 18, 1924, with Archbishop Alexander Rodostolou officiating.

In September 1954, Reverend Spyridakis retired, having served the Greek Orthodox community of St. Nicholas for thirty-six years as spiritual advisor and motivator. St. Nicholas needed to search for an equally far-sighted successor; their mission was accomplished by finding the young and energetic Reverend James A. Aloupis to become the spiritual leader of their beloved St. Nicholas Church.

Reverend George Spyridakis breaking ground on March 25, 1924, for the new St. Nicholas Greek Orthodox Church on High Street with members of the community.
Courtesy of Peter A. Adams

Afternoon Greek School students with their teacher, Mr. Pitouli, stand in front of the entrance to St. Nicholas Greek Orthodox Church on Academy Street, ca. 1910s.
Courtesy of St. Nicholas Greek Orthodox Church, Newark

At the conclusion of the first Divine Liturgy dedicating and consecrating the new edifice as an Orthodox Church on December 18, 1924, Archbishop Rodostolou and Reverend Spyridakis stand with some of the benefactors and their children in front of the *iconostasis* (icon screen).
Courtesy of the Adams and Pantages Families

Thyranoixia *(opening of the doors) for the building to become a place of Orthodox worship—the church was consecrated by placing a holy relic of St. Nicholas in the altar table and anointing the altar table with the Holy Chrism oil* (myron).

St. Nicholas Greek Orthodox Church celebrates its patron saint's day on December 6, ca. the 1960s. Clergy participating in the Artoklasia at the end of a vesper service on December 5 are, from left, Reverends Coutros, Aloupis, Zois, Condoleon, Gracias, and Mamangakis. Five loaves, symbolic of Jesus blessing the five loaves in the desert, are placed on a tray, along with the wine, oil, and wheat to be blessed.
Courtesy of St. Nicholas Greek Orthodox Church, Newark

I remember attending the Vesper service for St. Nicholas, December 5, 1942, with Archbishop Athenagoras officiating and air-raid sirens blaring. All the lights were put out in the church and the service continued.
JOHN F. POULOS

St. Nicholas was beautiful. I felt blessed and honored to be with Father Spyridakis. He was like a second father to me. On September 19, 1954, at my first sermon, with Father Spyridakis on my right, I told the congregation that above all is our love and respect for Father Spyridakis. Our hearts will always be open, our doors will always be open, and the love of St. Nicholas will always embrace you.
⌒ Reverend James A. Aloupis

Unlike most Greek Orthodox priests serving in the churches of the Americas, Father Aloupis was American-born, in Lynn, Massachusetts, and graduated from Bates College in Lewiston, Maine, and the Greek Theological Seminary in Pomfret Center, Connecticut. Raised by his family, who came from Sparta, Greece, he could understand the cultural complexities of both his Greek American parishioners and the metropolitan Newark neighboring areas.

With vigor and vitality, he (Aloupis) undertook all the tasks confronting him, including the spiritual and moral problems of much broader concept. Under Aloupis's leadership, the concept of the St. Nicholas family was applied to parish thinking.[7]
⌒ John Cunningham

Reverend James Aloupis was actively involved within the total community throughout his priesthood. At his first parish council meeting, Father Aloupis instituted his "good neighbor policy." He went to all the churches and synagogues in Newark to meet and work with clergy of all denominations. In addition, he visited hospitals in Newark and the neighboring areas to comfort the community at large. At the state level, he worked with Dave Warner, national director of the Boys' and Girls' Clubs of America. During this time, Father Aloupis was also appointed the national director of the Greek Orthodox Youth of America (GOYA), organizing chapters throughout the country.

I believe in being a good neighbor, not only with the Greek Orthodox communities, but also with the American community. I went to meet Mayor Carlin to discuss concerns about the city, county, and state. I told him that if at any time the local probation office had any problems with any Greek youngsters, to call me.
⌒ Reverend James A. Aloupis

In 1964, expansion of the church with a community center for the school and youth programs and other church organizations was undertaken. Groundbreaking took place on June 18, 1967, and in April 1969, His

Establishing Churches in Newark

Eminence Archbishop Iakovos of North and South America dedicated and officially opened the new Father Spyridakis Center.

From the beginning of his tenure, the community flourished with Father Aloupis, known in the larger community of New Jersey as the "Agape" priest. He believed and lived the word.

> *On the Sunday following the 1967 riots in Newark, the biggest parade of waves and waves of people marched on High Street. All these years I've been talking about "Agape"—what does it mean? Everyone left the church to go home, but I remained in the church. I opened all the doors and windows and stood in front of St. Nicholas. The parade started. I had never seen so many people. Two cars with police in them stopped in front. There I am smiling, and through a megaphone I heard, "Offer a prayer, Father, we need it." I offered a prayer and invited the people to come into the church. They came inside the church, not touching, not breaking anything, endless people. Two men approached me and wanted to know my reaction. I said that I had no regret but was honored and privileged to have these people enter the church, my one regret being that the Greek women had not prepared pastries and coffee for everyone. The next day the* New York Times *headline read, "Greek Priest Laments No Coffee for People." Something told me to do that.*
> ⌒ Reverend James A. Aloupis

Preparing for a Christian Unity Service on January 12, 1976, at St. Nicholas Greek Orthodox Church are, front row from left: Reverend James A. Aloupis of St. Nicholas; Mr. Tucker, president of the Metropolitan Ecumenical Ministry of Greater Newark; Reverend Robert Wardrop of the Ecumenical Commission of the Episcopal Diocese of Newark; and Reverend Robert Wood, pastor, Zion United Church of Christ of Newark. Behind them are Reverend John R. Sharp, moderator of the Presbyterian Church of Newark, and Father John Radano of Seton Hall University, member, Ecumenical Commission of the Archdiocese of Newark. ***Courtesy of St. Nicholas Greek Orthodox Church, Newark***

Dedicating the Reverend Spyridakis Hall of St. Nicholas Greek Orthodox Church, ca. 1970, are, from left, Maria Spyridakis Argyris, Reverend James A. Aloupis, and Maria A. Adams. The architect was William Chirgotis. ***Courtesy of St. Nicholas Greek Orthodox Church, Newark***

At the June 18, 1967, groundbreaking ceremonies for the St. Nicholas Greek Orthodox Church Community Center are, front row from left: Reverend Spyridakis, Metropolitan Silas, Mr. A. Argyris, Mayor H. Addonizio, Reverend J. A. Aloupis, Mr. L. Danzig, of the Newark Housing Authority, Parish Council President Mr. G. Maroulakos, and parishioners.
Courtesy of St. Nicholas Greek Orthodox Church, Newark

St. Demetrios Church

In 1928 a second church in Newark was established by a few Greek families originally from Chios and Mani. With the support of the Pansamian Society, they leased
a second-story flat at 120 Bank Street to serve as a church as well as a Greek school.
Reverend Nicholas Papademetriou became the first priest of the second Greek
Orthodox church in Newark, St. Demetrios.

St. Demetrios Greek Orthodox Church at
135 New Street, ca. 1932.
Courtesy of the Poutsiaka Family

> *I was seven years old when I got into trouble in church for chewing gum.*
> *Father Pappas called me into his office, made me spit out the gum, stand in*
> *front of the icon, and told me I was going to be an altar boy. That was the*
> *beginning of my involvement with the church. When Father went to homes*
> *to perform christenings, I would go with him carrying the Bible, icon, and*
> *blessed water. Someone would drive us, Father baptized the baby in a pan, and*
> *then we would go eat in the dining room. When I was twelve, I would get up*
> *at 5 a.m. to put coal in the stove to heat the church for Sunday services. The*
> *priest, at that time, only got $300 per month. He gave back about $100 of that*
> *because he did everything.*
> ☞ Gus Genakos

During this period, the Great Depression was beginning, and the spirit, deter-
mination, and faith of the congregants faltered because of the financial hardships
that followed. However, in 1932 the congregation purchased another building at
135 New Street with Reverend Papademetriou the spiritual leader of St. Demetrios
until his passing in 1952.

In 1947 they purchased the property at 210 Clinton Avenue. In 1952 Reverend
Christopher Condoleon assumed the spiritual guidance of St. Demetrios. The 1950s
and 1960s were years of progress and growth, reaching a membership of almost
five hundred families, with all the organizations and Greek and Sunday schools
achieving success.

With families becoming more affluent and the GI Bill after World War II providing
impetus for education and down payments for homes, the exodus from the environs
of Newark began. As the suburbs attracted families, other Greek Orthodox churches
established communities throughout the state. In the early 1970s, the social climate of
Newark began to change. As membership involvement in both the social and spiritual
activities began to decline, the need to relocate became evident. St. Demetrios Church
was the first to leave Newark and buy property on Rahway Avenue in Union, New
Jersey. The dedication service for their new church was held on October 14, 1984.

As for St. Nicholas, change is also a part of its continuing story. In 1998 the
membership decided to merge with the community of Sts. Constantine and Helen of
Orange and relocate to Roseland. Plans to build a new church in the Byzantine style
are now under way to give tribute to the unceasing efforts of the Greek immigrants
whose labors and sacrifices first created the "Mother Church of New Jersey."

St. Demetrios

Above: Altar boys at St. Demetrios Greek Orthodox Church, ca. 1945. Standing in front of the altar from left are: Artie Frangos, Gus Genakos, Father Nicholas Pappas, Tony Logothetis, and Tony Strobolakos.
Courtesy of Gus Genakos

Right: Reverend Nicholas Triandafilou was the second priest of the newly formed St. Demetrios Greek Orthodox Church on 120 Bank Street, ca. late 1920s.
Courtesy of Louis Triandafilou

Far right: Reverend Nicholas Papademetriou (Pappas), first priest of St. Demetrios Greek Orthodox Church, ca. 1940s. He left shortly after the church was founded but returned, remaining until the arrival of Reverend Christopher Condoleon.
Courtesy of Gus Genakos

Reverend Christopher Condoleon was the third priest to serve St. Demetrios Greek Orthodox Church, from 1952 to 1981. He was born on the island of Chios. His great grandfather, grandfather, and father all were priests. He was educated in the Rizarios Theological School in Athens and came to the United States in 1943.
Courtesy of Ona Frankos Spiridellis

The exterior of the newly renovated St. Demetrios Greek Orthodox Church at 210 Clinton Avenue, purchased in 1947.

Sacraments

Andrew and Ethel Georges are partaking of the non-sacramental wine known as the "common cup" from Reverend Spyridakis at their marriage ceremony, ca. 1946, in St. Nicholas Greek Orthodox Church. The common cup signifies that they agree to share the bitterness and sweetness of life, which they will invariably encounter in the future as husband and wife.
Courtesy of the Juvelis Family

Officiating at the April 28, 1946, wedding of Olga Boucouvalas and Constantine Macris at St. Nicholas Greek Orthodox Church is Reverend Spyridakis. The couple, led by the priest, follows the ancient and historic procession around the Holy Table in the Dance of Isaiah, symbolizing great happiness and exultation.
Courtesy of Olga Macris

Reverend Condoleon officiates at the wedding of Peter and Fredericka Thomas at St. Demetrios Greek Orthodox Church, ca. 1932. The *koumbaro* (best man) exchanges the crowns of the bride and groom, symbolizing that they will become king and queen of their home. The ribbon, which connects the crowns, symbolizes that the two are united into one in Christ.
Courtesy of Mary Thomas Marolakos

51

At the baptism of infant Pamela Marolakos at St. Demetrios Greek Orthodox Church ca. 1965 are godmother Helen Genakos, preparing to place holy oil on the infant before immersing her into the baptismal font, and Antoinette Genakos, with Reverend Christopher Condoleon officiating.
Courtesy of Mary Thomas Marolakos

Certificate of Birth and Baptism of Maria Spiridoulias from the Greek Archdiocese of North and South America. Maria was baptized at St. Nicholas Greek Orthodox Church, Newark, by the Reverend Thomas Papageorge, 1912.
Courtesy of Calomira Papageorge Canaris

After his ordination to the priesthood by Metropolitan Silas on December 31, 1995, Father George A. Xenofanes stands with his wife, Presbytera Xenofanes, His Grace the Metropolitan, and Reverend Aloupis at St. Nicholas Greek Orthodox Church, the church where Xenofanes' parents married and he was baptized.
Courtesy of Reverend George A. Xenofanes

Reverend Peter Kostakos gives Holy Communion to a parishioner during the Divine Liturgy at St. Nicholas Greek Orthodox Church, ca. 1990s. Father Kostakos was born and raised in Newark, ordained a deacon by Reverend Spyridakis at St. Nicholas, became a priest, and after his retirement, assisted Reverend Aloupis at church services.
Courtesy of St. Nicholas Greek Orthodox Church, Newark

The exterior of St. Nicholas Greek Orthodox Church at 555 High Street, now Martin Luther King Jr. Boulevard.
Courtesy of St. Nicholas Greek Orthodox Church, Newark

Father Aloupis presents Demi Lampros with an award from the Greek Orthodox Archdiocese honoring her twenty-five years of service as choir director, October 29, 1995.
Courtesy of St. Nicholas Greek Orthodox Church, Newark

Holding an icon of the Resurrection is the chanter, Mr. Nikitas Juvelis, with Reverend James Aloupis in front of the altar at St. Nicholas Greek Orthodox Church.
Courtesy of St. Nicholas Greek Orthodox Church, Newark

St. Nicholas

The altar of St. Nicholas Greek Orthodox Church, ca. 1990s.
Courtesy of St. Nicholas Greek Orthodox Church, Newark

Shown inside St. Nicholas Greek Orthodox Church, ca. 1990s, are the hand-carved wooden *kouvoukleon* (Christ's tomb)—sent from Greece and used at Good Friday services—and the baptismal font.
Courtesy of St. Nicholas Greek Orthodox Church, Newark

Stained glass windows depicting religious themes were donated by St. Nicholas Greek Orthodox Church parishioners in memory of their loved ones.

Courtesy of Kostas Diamandas

ΕΙΣ ΜΝΗΜΗΝ
...ΝΑΣΙΟΥ ΚΑΙ ΚΥΡΙΑΚΟΥΛΑΣ Π. ΑΔΑΜΟΠΟΥΛΟΥ

Ο ΧΡΙΣΤΟΣ ...ΑΤ Η ΣΑΜΑΡΕΙΤΙΣ

ΔΑΠΑΝΗ
ΑΙΚΑΤΕΡΙΝΗΣ ΕΛ ΜΠΙΛΙΑ

Easter

Reverend James A. Aloupis celebrates Palm Sunday, the beginning of Holy Week, at St. Nicholas Greek Orthodox Church, ca. 1999. *Courtesy of St. Nicholas Greek Orthodox Church, Newark*

At St. Demetrios Greek Orthodox Church, the women of the Philoptohos prepare for the Holy Friday Burial service. Standing around the *kouvoukleon* (Christ's tomb), ca. 1950s, with the *epitaphio* (Christ's shroud) lying within are from left, Reverend Christopher Condoleon, Euterpe Papatheodorou, Androniki Morikas, Mrs. Beretsos, Eugenia Platanos, Mrs. Coniaris, Jenny Poulos, and Reverend Nicholas Pappas.
Courtesy of Euterpe Papatheodorou

Some of my fondest memories were coming home from Easter midnight services and bringing our lighted candles.
DIANA STATHOPOULOS

Who can forget the Resurrection service at St. Nicholas with Father Spyridakis and subsequently Father Aloupis. The church was packed to overflowing with everyone in Easter finery. After Divine Liturgy, renewed and spiritually uplifted by the highest and most joyful of all holy day services, we would go home to enjoy Evelyn's Easter preparations.
ARTEMIS VARDAKIS

I remember when we were young kids and attended the Resurrection service, how difficult it was to stay awake until midnight while also holding a lighted candle. There were a few incidents, where youngsters dozed off and caused some singeing of clothing.
PETER J. METSOPULOS

At this *Anastasi* (Resurrection service), which takes place at midnight on Holy Saturday, the church is darkened to resemble the Tomb of Christ. Reverends Aloupis and Kostakos come out of the altar with lighted candles and proclaim, "Come receive the light and glorify Christ, who rose from the dead" as the light is given to the congregation and passed from person to person.
Courtesy of St. Nicholas Greek Orthodox Church, Newark

"*In all my years of serving the Lord and His Church, I have never been so deeply and personally moved as I was with your splendid Choir and Director.*"
His Beatitude Nicholas VI, Patriarch of Alexandria, at St. Nicholas Easter Resurrection services, April 6, 1980

3

Religious *and* Secular Greek American Organizations

The church served as the center of all aspects of the Greek community. The religious and administrative needs of the community were fulfilled by various organizations. As membership increased, additional organizations and societies formed to meet the fundraising and social needs surrounding the community. The Greek religious and cultural organizations were closely interrelated.

In America, mixed choirs accompanied the church service along with the chanter. At St. Nicholas, the choir and its choirmasters enjoyed an enviable reputation for excellence throughout their years of participation at church.

The early choirmasters, Nicholas Karlash and George Anastassiou in particular, were noted composers of the liturgy starting with the Byzantine modes and creating four-part harmony. They were followed by Demetre Criona, a brilliant tenor, who filled the church with professional voices such as Jack Arnold, a bass, Mrs. Criona, a Russian operatic soprano, and, on occasion, Nicolaos Moschona from the Metropolitan Opera. Mr. Criona was choirmaster for more than thirty years, and upon his passing, Demetra Lampros, one of his young soprano soloists, became choirmaster. Her service in the choir extended over fifty-four years, thirty-five of which were as choirmaster. Harriet Matheakis was the organist for thirty years until 1958, followed by George Cosmoglos, who lent his talents for the next forty-four years.

The St. Nicholas Greek Orthodox Church Choir, ca. 1935 with choirmaster Nicholas Karlash on the front steps of the church.
Courtesy of St. Nicholas Greek Orthodox Church, Newark

I lent my alto voice to the St. Nicholas choir for some fifteen years. Mr. Criona, with his brilliant operatic tenor voice, was our choirmaster, but Father Spyridakis, whose impatience with choir errors and crying children made for a bit of melodrama on a Sunday morn, often unnerved the poor man.
— Helen Galanoplos

The acolytes, or altar boys, were chosen by the priest to assist him with conducting the service. The priest trained them in the procedures and disciplined them very sternly. This often provided a training ground for future priests.

Father Spyridakis didn't want much smoke coming out of the incense burner,

and every now and then, if he scolded them for being late, the altar boys would take the incense, grind it down, and toss it on the burning charcoal before handing it to him so as he swayed it, the smoke would billow out.

   Kostas Diamandas

The *Katichitiko Scholio* (religious instruction classes) began as an after-school program for the children and eventually became Sunday School. This program was inaugurated at St. Nicholas by Mrs. Minnie Zois with Father Spyridakis in 1918.

We went to Sunday School, where we were taught our catechism in Greek. We went to Greek School every day after American school for some five years. I didn't like it at the time, except for the crazy shenanigans of some unruly students who will remain unnamed. Our teachers dealt with obstreperous students with a twelve-inch ruler on their knuckles.

   Helen Galanoplos

St. Nicholas Greek Orthodox Church choir members sing at a cutting of the *vasilopita* (St. Basil's Day cake) in the Father Spyridakis Hall. Around the table, from left, are: Demetre Criona, choirmaster, Marion Economo, Diana Stathopoulos, Marigo Markos, Barbara Zois, Demi Lampros, Reverend James Aloupis, Mrs. Kehayes, Philoptohos president, and George Maroulakos, president, Board of Trustees, ca. January 1970.
Courtesy of St. Nicholas Greek Orthodox Church, Newark

Students of St. Demetrios Greek Orthodox Church School ready to perform in a Christmas pageant ca. 1932–33 at the Ukranian Stritch Hall. First row from left: Andrew, Venetia, and Charles Coniaris. Second row: Manny Lamprou, Stella Sakelakos, Rose Billias, Mr. Karandreou, Harriet Vretos, Anthoula Koronakos, and Irene Pawlakos. Row three: Alice Pawlakos, Nick Lamprou, _____ Manos, Faye Chletsos, John Coniaris, and Honey Vretos.
Courtesy of the Coniaris Family

Our Greek school teacher was Mr. Karandreou. We would memorize Greek plays (ten to twelve pages long) and perform, even if we didn't know what the words meant, and present them to the community.
DR. CHARLES CONIARIS

The church also provided instruction in the Greek language. For the most part, these Greek language schools did not focus on religion, but rather taught the language and culture, including ancient Greek history and mythology.

> *Greek School had movable desks (which were pushed aside for church services), seating six or eight students. All classes were together, and the teacher would teach a class in front, then rotate the groups. It was a one-room schoolhouse, and everyone heard all the lessons taught. Our Greek schoolteacher was Mr. Pitouli.*
> ⌒ Joanna Gellas

> *We went to St. Nicholas Greek School and during exetases (end-of-the-year ceremonies), we all wore white and recited poems and performed Greek plays. The church sometimes used the Jewish YWHA, where we sang Greek and American national anthems.*
> ⌒ Helen Juvelis Calathos

The following poem reminded students in Greek school that under Turkish occupation, children continued their religious and cultural education and preserved the Greek language by secretly going to school at night.

Φεγγαράκι μου λαμπρό	*Oh, my bright and shiny moon,*
φέγγε μου να περπατώ	*Illuminate my path*
νά πηγαίνω στο σχολείο	*As I walk to school,*
να μαθαίνω γράμματα	*That I may learn to read and write:*
γράμματα σπουδάματα	*Learning and knowledge*
το Θεού τα πράγματα.	*And all of God's teachings and blessings.*

—Child's poem, author unknown. Translation with poetic license by Vasiliki G. Diamandas and Maria D. Yatrakis

Youth programs were also instituted as part of the church experience. During the 1940s, the two Newark churches had a combined youth group that met at St. Demetrios. It eventually became a part of the Greek Orthodox Youth of America, GOYA, which was established in 1951 under the auspices of the Greek Orthodox Archdiocese of North and South America. It was composed largely of young men and women between eighteen and thirty-five years of age. Committed to serving the church, "Goyans" were involved in religious education such as lectures, forums, retreats, and workshops. The GOYA motto was "Live Your Orthodox Faith."

Junior GOYA was a growing and fun experience. We had wonderful advisors, including our dear Father James A. Aloupis, who began all of our meetings with a prayer. As an officer in the organization, I learned to conduct meetings and organize fundraisers and dances with the Junior GOYAs of other Greek Orthodox churches. Throughout the state, Junior GOYA helped us all make lifelong friendships.

⤿ Barbara Christos Massad

As the American youth of Greek descent became actively involved in the public schools they attended, to support their interests such as sports, the Greek American Athletic Association (GAMAA) sponsored athletic events for their participation.

The Philoptochos, the ladies auxiliary, was the philanthropic arm of the church, sponsoring activities to raise money for church projects and particularly to provide for the needs of new immigrants and the indigent. In 1927, Minnie Zois of St. Nicholas organized a club for girls named *Proinia*, which means "we who help," the forerunner of the Philoptochos. Its mission was unity for the church and helpers of the poor. Marina Corodemus was another founding member of the St. Nicholas Ladies Philoptochos Society. Father Aloupis referred to her as the "Godmother of the St. Nicholas Philoptochos." The first president of the St. Demetrios Philoptochos was Mrs. Jenny Poulos, who was aptly called the "Mother of our Church." Mrs. Eufterpe Papatheodorou also served the society as its president, becoming one of the "godparents" of the new church in Union.

As the church developed, other organizations formed to enhance and support the cultural, social, and financial needs of the growing Greek American community. The ethnic groups continued assisting new immigrants and giving financial help to the villages and towns they had left through social events sponsored for this purpose. The church, with these groups and others established during this time, afforded all, particularly young people, an opportunity to meet other Greek Americans by sponsoring dances, dinners, and picnics.

The Greek American Progressive Association (GAPA), a national organization founded in 1923, focused on preserving the Greek Orthodox Church, the language, and traditions to counter the complete assimilation of Greek Americans into American culture.

We were a great group of girls in GAPA. . . . We did charitable works and had dances to raise money. I was both secretary and president of the organization and enjoyed it tremendously. We had great masquerade parties where we all dressed in beautiful costumes. For us at that time, it was a wonderful organization.

⤿ Mary Vasiliow Pantelis

Mrs. Minnie Zois is honored for her work with the Philoptochos by, from left, Reverend Aloupis, Metropolitan Silas, and President of the Board of Trustees Spyros Dendrinos, ca. 1950s.
Courtesy of St. Nicholas Greek Orthodox Church, Newark

> *I enjoyed my time in GAPA. We put on musical shows with various girls*
> *playing instruments. We went on picnic trips to Eagle Rock Mountain and to*
> *the Jersey shore. We were allowed to go because it was all girls.*
> Pipina Vasiliow Valauri

The American Hellenic Education Progressive Association, AHEPA, a national organization, was founded on July 26, 1922, in Atlanta, Georgia, in response to the "evils of bigotry and racism" that emerged in early-twentieth-century American society. It also helped Greek immigrants assimilate into society. Moreover, through the span of its history, AHEPA has served as a vital vehicle for the progressive development and emergence of American citizens of Greek heritage into every facet of society: government, businesses, education, and the arts.[8]

The Newark AHEPA chapter, Eureka 52, established in 1924, focused on assimilating into the American cultural and business community. It became the largest and most influential chapter in the Fifth District. In addition to social functions, Eureka 52, along with its auxiliaries, the Daughters of Penelope, Sons of Pericles, and Maids of Athena, has continuously supported philanthropic, educational, and political causes, both national and local, throughout the years.

> *The AHEPA was probably the second most important factor in Greek life. It afforded the opportunity to keep our heritage in the new country. It was an organization for Greek men. It was also the social mainstay of the Greek community. In addition to fundraising efforts during the war and throughout the years, the AHEPA held a large annual gala. People dressed in formal attire, and the dances were held at the finest hotels in Newark. Dancing to live Greek bands kept revelers well into the wee hours of the morning.*
> ⌒ Stella Visas Economo

All the organizations encouraged and promoted the Greek traditions, language, and culture. They celebrated ethnic holidays such as Greek Independence Day, March 25, when adults and children dressed in regional and classical Greek costumes.

> *We would get a haircut at Mr. Staikos's barbershop and then see him in an Evzone costume on Greek Independence Day at church services at St. Nicholas.*
> ⌒ John F. Poulos

Costumes were an integral part of Greek celebrations, as participation in multicultural and intercultural activities increased to foster understanding and fellowship with the ever-growing Greek American and American community.

The Theophiles children, Constantine with twins Angeliki and Angelo, pose in Greek costumes, ca. 1920s.
Courtesy of Perry P. Zagoreos

The students of the 1932 St. Nicholas Greek Orthodox Church School at end-of-year exercises standing on the steps of the church. *Courtesy of St. Nicholas Greek Orthodox Church, Newark.*

(Row 1) D. Stathopoulos, M. Polychronopoulos, M. Louvis, C. Karambelas, C. Koutsaftes, A. Malavazos, M. Pavlakos, H. Panagakos, Z. Petrou, P. Moutis, D. Lambros, A. Kallianes, M. Zizos, A. Linardakis, V. Corris, B. Panagakos, F. Evangelis, unknown

(Row 2) M. Bistis, B. Vlahos, G. Pavlakos, J. Koutsaftes, P. Jovanis, J. Corodemus, G. Stathopoulos, J. Karanasos, unknown, Liverakos, J. Polychondriotis, C. Polychondriotis, A. Koutsaftes, _____ Thophilos, J. Nikitakis, G. Moutis, B. Boutsikaris, B. Karanikolas, J. Vlastaras

(Row 3) H. Corodemus, B. Vlahou, K. Panagakos, _____ Liverakis, J. unknown, J. Karambelas, unknown, M. Mandas, S. Petrou, C. Jovanis, M. Dolias, unknown, N. Apostolakos, F. Karanasos, B. Pallantios, A. Churus, P. Pavlakos, unknown

(Row 4) P. Jovanis, J. Maroulakos, B. Chamouras, unknown, N. Sacclaris, unknown, J. Margeotis, A. Panagakos, J. Kafalas, P. Thomas, J. Theophilos, M. Pontiakos, G. Pallantios, G. Stephanis, unknown, N. Boutsikaris, A. Gianaras, _____ Vlahou, S. Papanicolaou, M. Sousanis

(Row 5) A. Johnson, unknown, S. Jemas, B. Lakos, A. Fillio, unknown, unknown, E. Lambros

(Row 6) unknown, J. Kapsimalis, P. Kapsimalis, _____ Bistis, P. Jaulis, G. Karanasos, E. Sarantos, K. Alevras, S. Aridas, G. Aridas, M. Mandas, A. Andrian, A. Apostolakos, unknown, M. Bistis

(Row 7) E. Adams, G. Andrian, unknown, J. Gianis, unknown, M. Stamatakos, unknown, N. Apostolinas, M. Gianaras, G. Zizos, J. Karonikolas, B. Morris, unknown, A. Zigopoulos, J. Johnson, G. Stamatakos, J. Zizos

A page taken from a Greek language alphabet book used by students of the afternoon Greek School classes; similar to the English *Dick and Jane* series used in elementary schools, 1946. Taken from the *Alphabet Book of the Greek Child of America*, D. C. Divry Inc., Publishers.
Courtesy of Helen Peters Cap

One cat with kittens.
Here is one large kitten, Nick.
Milk, kitten. Drink good milk.

Arranged on the steps of St. Nicholas Greek Orthodox Church are Sunday School students with Reverend Spyridakis in row 4, left; Deacon Kokinakis in row 4, right; and Mrs. Spyridakis, last row, right, ca. 1940. *Courtesy of John Shenis*

(Row 1) Unknown, Steve Diamandas, Peter Petropoulos, Bill Mavrode, Arthur Anest, Gus Diamandas, Leo Sirakedis, Nick Juvelis, Anthony Vlastaras, _____ Antonias, Marigo Pappas, Corinne Pappas, Anna Katsoris, Mary Demos, Esther Argyris, Ann Nikitakis, Bertha Panagakos, Mary Thomas, Helen Argyris, Esther Dokas, unknown

(Row 2) T. Papastavros, John Bravakis, John Antonakos, Spero Gevas, unknown, unknown, Gus Carumpalos, Tom Gevas, George Panagakos, Gus Karanicholas, John Shenis, Mary Karanasos, Fifi Prassas, Cathy Carumpalos, Sophie Micheludis, Aphrodite Kasmias, Angie Halamandaris, Jean Pontiakos, Doris Churus, Beatice Gevas, Cordelia Gevas

(Row 3) Unknown, Billy Theofilos, Jim Policantriotis, Jim Gevas, Arthur Carpousis, unknown, Stragalas, Dino Bliablias, unknown, George Zografos, Anna, unknown, unknown, Stragalas, unknown, Fotini _____, Percy Peters, Elaine Sideris, unknown, Pauline Stefanos, Penelope Pappas, Helen Sideris, unknown, Estelle Bravakis

(Row 4) Father G. Spyridakis, unknown, unknown, Ted Halamandaris, Jim Maroulakos, Chris Sirakedis, Steve Karas, Jim Pallantios, Peter Kapsimalis, Catherine Mandos, Mary Tomasco, Helen G., Eugenia Gevas, Betty Kafalas, Zoe Javas, Emorfia Gevas, unknown, Bertha Javas, Deacon Kokkinakis

(Row 5) Pete Thomas,_____ Karanasos, unknown, Steve Sgourakis, Steve Tsavlis, teacher _____, Athena Sarantos, Georgia Pagonis, Angie Juvelis, Olympia Zografos, unknown, unknown, unknown, Mrs. Spyridakis

I went to Greek School and Sunday School at St. Nicholas. My mother and father taught me some Greek reading and writing, so I started Greek School in the second grade. I was an altar boy for eight years. We had many Greek friends because the area around St. Nicholas was a Greek community.

NICHOLAS MICHELUDIS

In the winter on the way to Greek School, the boys would have snowball fights and be late for classes. Father Spyridakis would be waiting at the door with a big ruler and would ask all the boys to show their hands. If they looked cold or frostbitten, he would execute a slap on each hand (or more) for being late and not attending classes on time. In the warm weather, the boys often would try to play baseball rather than go to Greek School. Father Spyridakis would run through the neighborhood and gather them up for classes.

KOSTAS DIAMANDAS

Youth

Above and below: Friends belonging to the Hellenic Youth Organization formed in 1947 meeting at St. Demetrios Greek Orthodox Church on Clinton Avenue, ca. 1940s.
Courtesy of Pannoria Petine

Our Gang Baseball Club posing at Branch Brook Park Reservoir. In row 1 from left, third and fourth are Pete Mehalaris and Ted Lekas. In row 2 first, second, and third are Jim Balatsos, Charlie Coniaris, and Nick Billias. In row 3, third and fourth, are Pete Kostoulakos and Billy Chamouras, ca. 1936–37.
Courtesy of the Coniaris Family

Members of the St. Nicholas Greek Orthodox Church basketball team played in the Newark YMCA League, ca. 1950. Seated from left are Ernie Tsaptsinos, Nick Pilavakis, unknown, John Tsaptsinos. Back row from left: Coach Mike Karambatos, Tom Markos, George _____, and coach George _____.
Courtesy of St. Nicholas Greek Orthodox Church, Newark.

A GAMAA event, ca. 1960, honors Tom Manos for his work with community youth. From left are Mike Gargas; Barbara Zois; Dave Warner, president of the South Ward Boys Club; the honoree, Tom Manos; and Charles Kourebanas.
Courtesy of the Pallantios and Manos Families

Our summer entertainment was picnics. Few of us owned cars, and fewer owned houses with grounds. The families from various regions of Greece would each have their own picnic. Buses would be rented to transport the Greeks to their picnic venue, where there was always the enticing smell of Greek food and a live band providing Greek music for dancing.

HELEN GALANOPLOS

On Sundays during the summer in the 1930s, we would go by truck to Eagle Rock, or Petrillo's Grove in Kenilworth, for Kastaniotiko Club picnics. The trucks would be loaded with people and food and would leave from our store.

BERTHA PALLANTIOS MANOS

Societies

Right: Pansamian, compatriots from the island of Samos, enjoying the company of family and friends, ca. 1940s.
Courtesy of the Faraklas Family

Below: The fifth annual national convention banquet of the Pansamian Federation of America at the Hotel Douglas, September 6, 1953.
Courtesy of George Genute (Giannoutsos)

On Sundays in the summer, the Greeks would take buses from the corner of West Market and Bank Streets to Petrillo's Grove. Going on a picnic was a major undertaking—no coolers; full meals in pots, legs of lamb, salads, etc. [This] went on throughout the whole summer as each society had its own picnic.

KOSTAS DIAMANDAS

Father was a member of the Society of Epirotes, Anagenesis, a social organization of fellow Epirotes, which had staunchly supported efforts to reunite that part of Northern Epirus (passed to newly established Albania by the Entente in 1913) with the rest of Epirus and Greece. It also funded aid to Epirus during the war years and communist upheaval in Greece.

ARTEMIS VARDAKIS

GAPA

"LEMNOS" STUDIO
122 E. 42ND ST.
N.Y.C.

ΕΓΚΑΘΙΔΡΥΣΙΣ ΤΩΝ ΑΞΙΩΜΑΤΟΥΧΩΝ
ΤΩΝ ΣΤΟΩΝ
ΙΠΠΟΚΡΑΤΗΣ ΜΕΡΙΜΝΑ, ΑΥΡΑ, ΚΑΙ ΔΕΛΦΟΙ
ΤΗΣ ΟΡΓΑΝΩΣΕΩΣ G.A.P.A.
ΜΑΡΤΙΟΥ 11-1936 ΤΟΥ NEWARK N.J.

Installation of the newly elected officers of GAPA, Newark Chapter, Hippocratis Lodge #57,
Avra and Delphi, March 11, 1936.
Courtesy of Mary Pantelis, Pipina Valauri, Louise Vasiliow

Sisters Pipina and Mary Vasiliow
pose in costumes prior to attending a
GAPA masquerade ball, ca. 1930s.
Courtesy of the Lampros Family

Chris Vasiliow and his uncle, Evangelos Nikitakis, are dressed as
Evzones, Greek royal honor guards. Mr. Nikitakis was president of
GAPA, Hippocratis Lodge #57, Newark, ca. 1940s.
Courtesy of the Lampros Family

Mrs. Militinis, representing all mothers and as president of the
Newark Chapter Avra, receives a bouquet of flowers from Hippocratis
Lodge #57 President Evangelos Nikitakis, and Chris Argyris
representing the veterans, ca. 1940s.
Courtesy of Mary Pantelis, Pipina Valauri, Louise Vasiliow

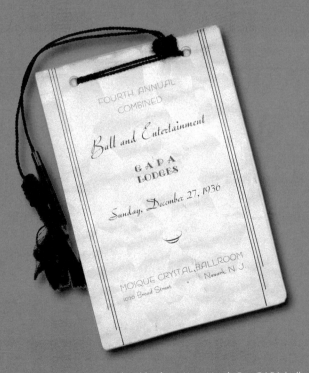

The cover of a program booklet for a New Year's Eve GAPA ball at the
Mosque Theater, December 1936.
Courtesy of Mary Pantelis, Pipina Valauri, Louise Vasiliow

АНЕРА

Above: AHEPA members and families attend the fifth annual picnic, Eureka Chapter 52, Order of AHEPA, July 31, 1932.
Courtesy of Theodore John Bravakis

Right: Officers of Eureka Chapter 52, Order of AHEPA. Seated from left are: George Visas, Sotirios Chiminidis, Steve Karkakis, and William Chirgotis. Standing are Tom Manos, Frank Zigopoulos, Gus Patrakis, William Economides, George Kacandes, Bobby Aridas, and Nick Javas, ca. 1930s.
Courtesy of the Pallantios and Manos Families

Martirika *are the small lapel ribbons with either a cross or religious medal, printed with the child's name, birth and baptismal dates, plus the godparents' names and the church, given to those witnessing the sacrament.*

COURTESY OF GEORGE C. PAPPAS

Eureka Chapter 52, AHEPA administration. First row, from left: George Visas, treasurer, George Lollos, William Economides, Steven Kargakos, vice president, William Chirgotis, secretary, Louis Kitsos, and Constantine Gevas. Standing are E. Belasco, Constantine Petrakis, Soterios Chiminidis, Frank Zigopoulos, George Kacandes, Spiro Givas, George Bravakis, Thomas Argyris, Nicholas Javas, O. Verres, Thomas Manos, and Theodore Bravakis, ca. 1940.
Courtesy of Theodore John Bravakis

George Lollos, president of Eureka Chapter 52, stands next to a wreath of flowers he designed in honor of AHEPA, ca. 1920s.
Courtesy of John Lollos

Martirika from Chrysanthe Lollos's baptism.
Courtesy of George C. Pappas

AHEPA was a big part of my father's life. He was president of Eureka Chapter 52. My sister Chrysanthe's middle name is legally AHEPA because Eureka Chapter 52 christened her when Dad was president. Therefore, every member of the AHEPA from that year is her godfather.

JOHN LOLLOS

Maria Hallax Pouliot, a Maid of Athena, performs the Charleston for the audience at the AHEPA Jubilee Convention in the Continental Ballroom, ca. 1949.
Courtesy of the Faraklas Family

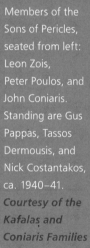

Members of the Sons of Pericles, seated from left: Leon Zois, Peter Poulos, and John Coniaris. Standing are Gus Pappas, Tassos Dermousis, and Nick Costantakos, ca. 1940–41.
Courtesy of the Kafalas and Coniaris Families

BASKETBALL AND DANCE

sponsored by

Corinthian Chapter 20

Sons of Pericles   Newark, New Jersey

to be held on

Sunday, January 16th, 1938

Cover of a 1938 Basketball/ Dance Journal of the Sons of Pericles.
Courtesy of Tom Demery (Tassos Dermousis)

We had a strictly Greek life. There was very little dating, always observing religious holidays. I remember back to a wonderful people where material things were not important—family was.
MARIA HALLAX POULIOT

Top: Maids of Athena, 1949. Seated left to right are: Mary Faraklas, Eugenia Gevas, Beatrice Gevas, Mary Hallax, Penny Kounelias, Jean Aridas, Zoe Javas, Helen Galanoplos, Estelle Bravakis, _____ Sideris, Elaine Anest, Mary Caranasos, Sophie Kostakis; standing: Irene Lellos, _____ Johnson, Esther Dokas, Betty Daniskas, unknown, unknown, Mary Nicholas, unknown, Corinne Maskaleris, unknown, Mary Thomas, unknown, unknown, unknown, _____ Aritakis, unknown, Frances Gallos, Helen Peters, unknown, Stella Corodemus, Angie Terzakos.

Bottom: Daughters of Penelope, women's auxiliary Order of AHEPA, new member party, ca. 1940s. From left in row 1: Carol George, Ruth Galanopoulos, _____ Cocoris, Bess Arbes, Alice Bravakis, Olga Chiplakes, Ida Theoharis, Bertha Manos, Dot Theoxalis, Sophie Bravakis, Mary Gerakos; Row 2: _____ Nicholas, Helen Chirgotis, Jean Aridas, Pat Paskas, Theda Manos, Jean Galanopoulos, Irene Gines, Jean Chirgotis, Ann Bravakis, Sophie Javas.
Courtesy of the Pallantios and Manos Families

Left: The ladies of St. Demetrios Greek Orthodox Church, some in Amalia costumes, with Reverend Nicholas Pappas prior to marching in the Holy Cross Parade in Atlantic City, ca. 1940s.
Courtesy of the Coniaris Family

Right: The Coniaris children, from left: Andrew, Venetia, and Charles, with John's arms around his brothers' shoulders. The boys are dressed in Evzone costumes, ca. 1935.
Courtesy of the Coniaris Family

Costumes

Marie Johnson (Adams) in patriotic costume holding the American flag on Greek Independence Day, ca. 1917.
Courtesy of Adams and Pantages Families

The Jolas twins, Constantine and Pauline, appear in Greek village costumes, ca. 1930s.
Courtesy of Jolas Family

This Greek dance group includes, from top left, Mary Thomas, Helen Tsaolis, Bertha Polychrony, Evelyn Petropoulos. Kneeling from left, Olga Kefalas, Sylvia Kefalas, and Helen Polychrony in Amalia costumes, the Royal Court attire of Queen Amalia, ca. 1950s.
Courtesy of Mary Thomas Maroulakos

Chrysanthe and Betty Lollos in Greek costumes, ready to participate in the Greek parade, ca. 1940s.
Courtesy of John Lollos

Spiro, in Evzone costume, is with his siblings George, Catherine, and Peter Poulos, ca. 1930s.
Courtesy of Spiro Poulos

Phil and Jim Gevas in a typical portrait taken at the Kapetan Studio. Phil is wearing an Evzone costume, the proudest symbol of Greek manhood and Greek martial nobility and history, ca. 1930s.
Courtesy of the family of Constantine and Olga Gevas

In less than a half-century, the contributions of the Greek American community of Newark and surrounding areas were enormous because of individual and group efforts. One by one, contributions, both great and small, added to the pride of Newark's and New Jersey's Hellenic sons and daughters.
Charles F. Cummings, Newark
City historian

4

Businesses and Professions

By the 1920s, the Greek entrepreneurial spirit, energy, and desire to succeed led to the establishment of a variety of businesses.

> *Anthony Javas came to the United States at the age of nineteen or twenty. One day he walked from Jersey City into Newark and passed a bakery on Lombardy Street. He was hungry, and asked for a slice of bread to eat. He was refused the bread, and as he left, he told himself that one day he would buy that bakery, and anyone who asked for some bread would never be refused. He held true to his promise. After first opening a bakery on Lock Street with his brothers, Peter and Michael, he finally did buy the bakery on Lombardy Street.*
>
> ~ Helen Angelides

Businesses

From pushcarts to elegant restaurants, businesses such as barbershops, tailors, food establishments, and wholesale enterprises began to flourish. These enterprises spread throughout Newark, bringing closer contact with the public.

This photograph of Market Street (1908) reflects the types of businesses that Greeks operated.
Courtesy of The Newark Public Library

The Paramount Food Market was run by Mr. Pallantios, then by Tommy and Bertha Manos, who inherited the market from Bertha's father.

It was a wonderful market [on West Market Street], with its butcher shop in the rear of the store, taken care of by Tommy, and the groceries and loose spices in the front of the shop giving off a wonderful aroma, overseen by Bertha.
  Reverend George A. Xenofanes

My father was working for Psihoghis, who had a fruit stand on Broad Street near Commerce. Next door was a restaurant owned by a Greek who got me a job with a relative at a hot dog stand in Rye Beach, New York. I went to work for him in the summer, washing dishes, helping sell hot dogs . . . yelling, "Red hot franks, ice cold lemonade and orangeade, come and get it!"
  William Chirgotis

From 1920 through 1950, Greeks owned 65 percent of the food businesses in downtown Newark. The Central Bar and Grill, owned by Angelo Peters in the 1920s, was located at 199 Wright Street in Newark in the farmer's market and industrial area at the south end of Broad Street. The restaurant was bought by the Vardakis family in 1935.

My father's customers were a colorful mix of wholesalers, factory executives, factory workers, bookkeepers, farmers, health inspectors, and truck drivers. Father took pride in owning that store with its broad front windows, blocked terrazzo floor, marble tabletops, and beautifully framed art-deco mirrors covering one entire wall.
  Artemis Vardakis

In 1920 Nick and John Faraklas incorporated the Aroma Coffee Company.

They rented the first floor at 120 Bank Street, Newark, eventually buying the building under the name Faraklas Realty Company. They bought raw coffee beans, mostly from South America and some from Africa, and would roast, grind, and do their own blends, packaging them in one-pound bags. The brothers would sell them, along with tea, spices, and other restaurant supplies, wholesale to restaurants and diners all over New Jersey and parts of New York and Pennsylvania.
  Mary Faraklas Diamandas

Greeks became owners of barbershops, hat cleaning and blocking, shoe repair, and tailor businesses.

In the [U.S.] Army, wanting to learn another trade, Spiro reminded his superior officer that Greeks were also expert tailors. Since all of the uniforms were tailor-made, he found his calling. This was to be his trade for the rest of

Standing in front of the Paramount Food Market at 83 West Market Street are proprietors Tom and Bertha Manos, ca. 1939.
Courtesy of the Pallantios and Manos Families

George Petropoulos, proprietor, outside the Central Coffee Pot Restaurant, located in the Newark Farmer's Market, 1936.
Courtesy of Helen Peters Cap

My father was the sole owner of the Central Coffee Pot Restaurant. He owned this restaurant for about thirty-five or forty years. It was originally located at 11 Joseph Street, Newark Farmers Market. At the same time my father owned this business, from 1936 to 1939, he partnered with my uncle, Angelo Petropoulos and my godfather, Theodore Pantos, building the Palomar, a first-class restaurant attached to the Wiss Building. The entrance, I believe, was on the side street (Park Street), and it had bronze columns designed after Longchamps. It eventually became the gift shop for Wiss Jewelers. The economy of the 1930s forced the closing of this restaurant.

HELEN PETERS CAP

George Petropoulos looking out the window of the Central Coffee Pot Restaurant.
Courtesy of Helen Peters Cap

his life. . . . [After the war] he opened a tailor shop in Newark's Roseville section on Orange and Fourth Streets, where he employed up to ten designers, fitters, and tailors.
Chrysanthy Kehayes Grieco

Printing and stationery enterprises were lucrative, addressing the needs of the various businesses. E. N. Plates Stationery was the major paper supplier of Newark's government agencies. B & B Press, opened in 1918 by

Constantine Bistis, began by serving the well-known Greek businesses of New Jersey.

> *When I was about ten years old, my brother got me a job at B & B Press delivering menus. They were very good to me. Mr. Bistis would give me 50 cents to have lunch for 25 cents at the Presto Restaurant and bring back the change. Then he sent me to linotype school in Brooklyn. I loved the machine and that shop.*
> ⌒ **Theodore J. Bravakis**

Others began collecting evergreens and flowers, eventually opening nurseries and florist shops.

> *In 1920 my father came to Newark to open the first wholesale evergreen business. No one at that time was in that type of business, so he opened Poulos Brothers (Peter and Chris Papanikolopoulos) on New Street. Father died a year later from TB, in 1921. He left the business to his wife, but her brother-in-law ran it. She helped in the business until 1932–33, when they went bankrupt.*
> ⌒ **Spiro Poulos**

> *My father came to Newark in the early 1920s. He went to work for the Washington Florist, which was owned by William Zois. At the time, the only greens they used were laurel, which was all over New Jersey. Kiddingly, they told my father to get his driver's license and they would give him an old truck and he could, on the side, collect laurel for them. So he did get his license, and he worked with them for a while. Later, my father opened his own wholesale evergreen business.*
> ⌒ **William Mavrode**

Some, having learned the fur trade in Greece or as apprentices in the United States, became furriers. Women, for the most part, entered retail sales markets or held secretarial positions, although the majority worked with their husbands or in their homes.

Women also ventured into the business world. Esther Argyris Chrisicos owned a lingerie shop on Broad Street in the early 1930s. Katherine Pantages was a candy buyer for L. Bamberger & Co. for many years. Clare Karambelas was manager of Wiss Jewelers on Broad Street. Many worked for the telephone company, Prudential Insurance, and other firms in downtown Newark.

> *My grandmother, who brought my mother and her six siblings from Greece, settled in Newark, where [she] earned income as a*

Nick and John Faraklas in front of their business, the Aroma Coffee Company, at 120 Bank Street in Newark, ca. 1950s.
Courtesy of the Faraklas Family

> *My father, Nikita Juvelis, took correspondence courses in English, finance, and sales. He received his diploma in 1918. He established the N. Juvelis Coffee Company in 1931, and his son, Stelios, took over the family business in 1970. They sold coffee, tea, and restaurant supplies.*
> HELEN JUVELIS CALATHOS

B & B Press, owned by the Bistis brothers, was one of the first printing businesses in Newark, ca. 1920s.
Courtesy of the Bistis Family

I went to Essex County Vocational School for printing. I went to linotype school in Brooklyn and started working for B & B Press. Later, I went into partnership with Nick Bistis when B & B separated. I went into the service, then went to work for Merit Press, which was owned by Theodore John Bravakis.
SPIRO POULOS

midwife. Mother went to Drake's Business School and became a legal secretary working for a law firm in Newark.
◦— Ileana N. Saros

When I was in high school, it was wartime, and I worked at the telephone company to replace the men who were in the service. I also was a secretary at the Essex County Courthouse, where I met my husband.
◦— Effie Maskaleris Vlahakes

About one-quarter of the partnerships in business were with relatives, compatriots, and friends, therefore receiving even more support from the immediate vicinity.

My father, together with his brothers, established the Broad and Market Music Company around 1910 at 163 Market Street in Newark in the newly constructed, two-story Prudential Building. It started as a Christmas card store, and over the many years turned into a complete music store selling records, sheet music, piano

The Old Newark Theatre on Broad Street as it was before Adam A. Adams bought it. A few doors to the left, one can see the sign of E. N. Plates' stationery store, ca. 1920.
Courtesy of the Adams and Pantages Families

rolls, phonographs, then on to the sale of radios, televisions, and appliances. As the music store business grew, diversified, and prospered, it became a landmark and the popular meeting place of recording, singing, and theatrical artists.

◔⁓ **Thomas A. Argyris**

A prominent Greek executive who owned and operated all the city's great movie palaces was Adam A. Adams (Adamopoulos). According to articles written about him, his was a "Horatio Alger" success story. Born in Greece, he landed on Ellis Island at the age of fourteen. He rose from immigrant shoeshine boy to owner of a chain of movie theaters in Newark and other areas of New Jersey. In 1915 he and his brother purchased the old Newark Theatre, renaming it the Paramount in 1931. In 1935 he purchased the Schubert Theatre, renaming it the Adams. Mr. Adams always helped the young men and women of Greek descent, hiring the men (including his sons) as ushers for $18 to $20 a week to start, then promoting them to head usher, captain, and eventually manager as they worked their way through school. The young women worked as cashiers and in the concessions. He was a major fund-raiser for St. Nicholas Church and the Newark community, and American and Greek charities acknowledged him for his philanthropic endeavors.

James Nicholas was the manager of the Adams Theatre, which was owned by his brother-in-law, A. A. Adams. Just about every young Greek man became an usher and held down the responsible and respected position. At one time, Jerry Lewis was an usher there, but James Nicholas was forced to fire him because of all his antics and cut-ups. All the big bands played there, with a new show coming every Thursday, at which time most of the high schools emptied out and everyone played hooky to see the new live show. Many of the Greek girls worked as cashiers at the theaters.

◔⁓ **Constance Nicholas Krentz**

Professionals

As the Greeks established financial stability, education became the priority for their children. Many in the first and second generation of Greek Americans were encouraged to enter various professions. Both men and women graduated into the fields of medicine, law, architecture, engineering, education, and the arts.

Dr. Nicholas Antonius, born in Greece and raised in Orange, New Jersey, began his medical career as an intern at St. Michael's Hospital in Newark. He opened an office in 1924 at 27 West Market Street and served the

The Washington Florist was established in 1906 at 577 Broad Street at the corner of Central Avenue. Six years later, it moved into a new building at 569 Broad Street. In 1912 it advertised that it was the largest retail florist in the state of New Jersey, ca. 1920.
Courtesy of Leon Zois and Family

My brother, Frank, and I established the Arcadia business in 1946 after having worked for the Washington Florist.
WILLIAM ZERVAKOS

The Lollos Florist, Inc., owned and operated by George Lollos, was located at 233–235 South Orange Avenue at the corner of Bergen Street, ca. 1930.
Courtesy of John Lollos

When my father saw my mother, who was living with the Gavalas family (relatives) in Spring Lake, he liked her. He was told he couldn't court her because he didn't have a business. So he started the flower business in order to marry her. He began by sweeping the floor of a florist on Park Avenue, learned the business, became a good designer, and opened a shop on Broad Street in Newark. In order to raise his family in the country, he built a larger shop ten years later at South Orange Avenue and Bergen Street. He had wealthy clients. He did floral arrangements for Mrs. Worthington's parties. She and others like her moved in the late 1940s, but his old customers were "friends," so our truck would deliver her weekly centerpieces to her home in Basking Ridge until she passed away.
JOHN LOLLOS

Greek American and American communities as a family doctor, helping many patients without concern for their ability to pay for his services. Dr. Antonius went on to become an eminent cardiologist, lecturer, and author, and Medical Director of St. Michael's Hospital.

> *My son, born prematurely, remained in the hospital for three months under the care of Dr. Antonius, who did not expect him to live. My wife would go to the hospital to give her milk and blood to try to help him survive. Dr. Antonius continued to take care of him and visit him at home occasionally, even in a snowstorm. When we went to pay him, he would not take any money, not even a penny.*
> **George Mendrinos**

Other doctors following his example included Dr. John Coniaris, who worked with Dr. Antonius, Dr. Malavazos, and Dr. Peter Poulos. Dr. Poulos first became an engineer, then a doctor specializing in thoracic surgery, and finally got a law degree so he could defend himself in a malpractice suit, which he won. Dr. Charles Coniaris was an optometrist, and his brother, Andrew, was a pharmacist. The first Greek pharmacist in the community was Mr. Papadopoulos. Dr. Critidis practiced dentistry, and Dr. Aridas was a chiropractor. More and more young men and women went into the medical profession in later generations.

Thomas A. Argyris and Louis Pantages were two of the many who received law degrees. Tom served as general counsel and vice president of Prudential

Katherine Pantages in the showroom placing an order for L. Bamberger & Co., ca. 1970s.
Courtesy of Katherine Pantages

Insurance, Newark, and for a period of time, he served as the municipal judge in Springfield in Union County. Louis Pantages represented insurance companies and became proficient in litigation and trial work.

The fields of architecture and engineering were also prominent in the career choices of young Greek Americans. William Chirgotis became a very well known architect, but never lost sight of his roots. He felt it was a privilege to support the Greek community. He designed the new social hall of St. Nicholas Church and served as the supreme president of the AHEPA.

> *I was fortunate enough to have a teacher at Central Avenue High School who took an interest in me and recommended I go to college for architecture. My father, at that time, didn't have two nickels to put together. He had to raise five kids. My instructor told me about a school in Brooklyn, subsidized by Mr. Pratt, which taught architecture and interior design. I took a two-day exam, was interviewed, and accepted. After World War II, returning soldiers and their families had no place to live, so it was easy for me to get financing to build apartments. And that's how my business started.*
> ❧ **William Chirgotis**

Angelina Halamandaris Aretakis pursued a career in engineering and was one of the first women to break the barrier of a male-dominated field.

> *I was the first Greek American woman to go to Newark College of Engineering. Although I received a scholarship for Rensselaer College, I was not permitted to live away from home because I was a girl. I received numerous awards, including the Tau Beta Pi Award (honorary engineering), given to very few women at that time.*
> ❧ **Angelina Halamandaris Aretakis**

Women entered the field of education. Among those becoming teachers were Olga Boucouvalas Macris, Joanna Gellas, Dot DeNicholas Bisbas, and Corinne Pappas Maskaleris, who later became an attorney.

> *My father sent me to Rider College, which had a very good teacher-training education program, and Father had a first cousin living there. I did have difficulty getting a job because I was handicapped from a childhood accident, which occurred when I was ten years old, in 1922. The infection in my bone caused my handicap even though they saved my leg.*

A Greek dance performed at the Griffith Building on Broad Street by, from left, Elinore Saratoes, Kay Tsotakos, Ethel Juvelis, and Eva Halulakos. Mr. Adam A. Adams donated the classical Greek costumes, June 1936.
Courtesy of the Juvelis Family

> *I played the clarinet, and my brother, George, and my cousin, Spiro Poulos, played the trumpet. Our lessons at Robbie's Music School cost $5 per lesson. The school was located in the Griffith Building on Broad Street next to Hahne's & Company.*
> WILLIAM MAVRODE

John Mehalaris plays his mandolin, ca. 1920s. Music was always part of every Greek home, and everyone was encouraged to play an instrument.
Courtesy of Peter Mehalaris

My mother, Christine Pappas, would take us to the World's Fair in 1939. We often stayed at the Greek pavilion. She often carried her mandolin and played it.
CORINNE PAPPAS MASKALERIS

Father had connections at City Hall, and he arranged for me to take an exam for teacher/clerk, and I came out third. I substituted and eventually got a full-time position as a teacher, where I remained for forty years.
— Joanna Gellas

The Great Depression

The Great Depression of the 1930s affected all economic classes the world over, bringing massive unemployment to both city and rural areas. Ethnic enclaves like the Greek community in Newark were not exempt. The Great Depression not only caused an economic upheaval for business, but it also caused a shift in family stability.

The Depression was very difficult, but everyone was in the same environment. I was thirteen years old and worked after school delivering Greek newspapers for Mr. Dermousis. I did this for three years, working from 3:30 until 6:30 every night, seven days a week for $3 cash. I would go downtown to Broad and Market Streets to the Argyris Appliance Store to give them the $3 each week for a refrigerator for my mother. It took me three years to pay it off. We didn't know what poor was. They call it the "good old days," but they were not "good old days." There was no food, stockings were mended, blisters on feet, froze in winter, and sweated in summer. It toughened us up and made us stronger.
— Dr. Charles Coniaris

The Potami Grocery Store, located at 64 Howard Street, was owned by the Kapandais Family. Front row from left: John, Kalliope, Garifalia, Angeliki Kapandais, Argio Platos, and Sophia Kapandais. Row 2: George and his mother, Maria Kapandais, and Gramatiki Borgias, ca. 1937.
Courtesy of Garifalia Kapandais Mellas

We were destitute, but had a happy life. We sat on the steps of the apartment building and talked. We played instruments; dad played guitar, I played harmonica, and we would sing at night. We didn't have much money, but it was pleasant.

⟳ James Petine

A few businesses actually survived the Depression, helping other family members, friends, and neighbors within the community.

During the Depression, the coffee company did very well as it was cheaper for folks to get a cup of coffee than a meal. On the other hand, the company did suffer many bad debts from folding businesses. Nick and John helped a lot of members of the Greek community financially during this time.

⟳ Mary Faraklas Diamandas

When I was fourteen, it was the peak of the Depression (1930). I was lucky to get a part-time job after school as a helper at the Boston Candy Store, which served the finest homemade ice cream and chocolates. The owner was Mr. Lampros.

⟳ Peter L. Vlahakes

During the Depression, Maria and Costa (Costandino) Kapandais started a store called Potami Grocery. This was the way they helped others and our family survive.

⟳ Garifalia Kapandais Mellas

In the first half of the twentieth century, the American spirit was emulated through the sacrifices made by the ethnic minorities at that time. These groups worked long hours at menial jobs with low pay to achieve economic success. Likewise, the Newark Greek community was a prime example of how an ethnic neighborhood offered opportunities to newly arrived compatriots, both socially and economically, which they may not have otherwise received if they had been totally immersed in the greater U.S. society. By helping each other to establish themselves in Newark, they were able to support the assimilation of other immigrants into the U.S. mainstream.

Dr. John Kallas grew up in Newark as the son of immigrant Greek parents. He is a Greek American author and playwright whose stories include the immigrant experience in Newark as he lived it as a boy.
Courtesy of the Kallas Family

Growing Up As A Greek-American

by Dr. John L. Kallas

Miss Angelina Halamandaris became Tau Beta Pi Women's Badge wearer No. 101 at a banquet given on November 22 by New Jersey Gamma. The badge was presented to her by Dr. C. A. Mantell, chairman of the chemical engineering department at the Newark College of Engineering. In presenting the badge, Dr. Mantell pointed out that Miss Halamandaris was about to join the few women who had invaded another of the so-called male professions and, through their ability and integrity, made their presence in engineering known. A senior in chemical engineer, Miss Halamandaris is a native of Paterson, N.J., and was graduated from Westside High School in Newark, where she received a Bausch and Lomb Science Award. She is active in the student branch of the American Chemical Society, secretary of the student chapter of the A.I.Ch.E., features editor of the *Yearbook*, and she writes a column for the school newspaper.

Angelina Halamandaris was honored at a banquet given on November 22 by NJGAMMA, ca. 1950s.
Courtesy of Angelina Halamandaris Aretakis

After becoming an attorney, my father had his practice in Newark for approximately sixty years. From 1962 to 1970, he served as Deputy Attorney General to the Professional Boards with an office in Newark.

ILEANA N. SAROS

Businesses

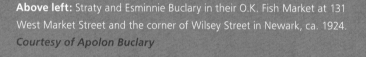

Above left: Straty and Esminnie Buclary in their O.K. Fish Market at 131 West Market Street and the corner of Wilsey Street in Newark, ca. 1924.
Courtesy of Apolon Buclary

Above right: James and Efstathia Demas are in front of their deli on High Street. The store was next to St. Nicholas Greek Orthodox Church, ca. 1940.
Courtesy of the Demas Family

Right: Friends meeting in front of the Liberty Food Market on West Market Street are, from left, Mickey Argyros, Steve Diamandas, the owner's son, Nick Linardakis, and Ted Faraklas, ca. 1950.
Courtesy of the Linardakis Family

They worked hard and long hours at the meanest occupations. Spiro's children, John and Matina, hardly ever saw their father and their Uncle John, who lived with them. They had gone to work by the time the children awoke and did not return from work before they had gone to bed.
JOHN ANTONAKOS

My family opened their store, Liberty Food Market (aka the Greek Store), on West Market Street in 1950.
KOSTAS DIAMANDAS

Above: Katherine Chletsos, in her family's Lemnos Bakery, preparing loaves of bread that are later blessed, broken into small pieces, and distributed to the parishioners after the Divine Liturgy service on Sundays in church, ca. 1945.
Courtesy of the Newark Public Library

Above right: Anthony Javas, proprietor of the Holsum Bakery, ca. 1950s.
Courtesy of Helen Angelides

Right: Tony Vlahakes delivering milk and food products to customers, ca. 1940s.
Courtesy of the Vlahakes Family

My father was a bread salesman all through the Depression years, serving the Greek community faithfully, and during this time providing them with bread on a "pay you later" basis. He worked for the Lemnos Bakery, located on Warren Street. He also got involved with the floral business, traveling often into the mountains to collect the necessary ferns that were part of floral arrangements.
JOHN KORONAKOS

There were three Greek bakers in Newark: Lemnos, located on Warren Street, owned by the Chletsos family; The Holsum Bakery, located on Lombardy Street, owned by the Javas brothers; and the Olympia Bakery, located on Lock Street, owned by the Perylis family.
PETER MEHALARIS

Inside George's Restaurant, at 85 Halsey Street, are Mr. Capetanos, left foreground, and Mrs. Capetanos at the back, ca. 1930.
Courtesy of Tom Capetanos

John Jolas in his hot dog store, located on the corner of Market Street and Raymond Boulevard. From left are John Jolas and his brother-in-law, George Pappas (George made all the candles for the Greek churches), ca. 1920s.
Courtesy of the Jolas Family

Mr. and Mrs. Moutis inside their South Park Restaurant, located on Broad Street, ca. 1950s.
Courtesy of George Moutis

Peter Moutis with his brother, Nicholas, and brother-in-law, Harry Panagakos, bought the South Park Restaurant on the corner of Broad and Chestnut Streets in 1918 for $700. As a waiter in other restaurants, he saved money to buy his own. They struggled through the Depression, and in 1952, he turned over the business to his son, George, daughter, Helen, and her husband, Lee Tsairis.

John Christos is standing behind the counter in his Atlantic Coffee Pot Luncheonette, June 18, 1951. *Courtesy of the Christos Family*

Friends Helen Halakos, Pauline Halakos, and Helen Halakos Kostas meet in front of Tuffy's Restaurant, ca. 1953.
Courtesy of Dessa Halakos Weiss

Kanella and Thomas Nagnostopoulos and their niece, Honey, in front of Thomas Greek Restaurant, ca. 1940.

Sam Markos is preparing food on the grill in his New Adelphia Restaurant at 320 Market Street, ca. 1952.
Courtesy of the Sam Markos Family

The L & M Luncheonette, owned by Sam Markos, on McCarter Highway and Commerce Street, ca. 1957.
Courtesy of the Sam Markos Family

An Easter display of homemade chocolate goodies is visible in the window of Chris' Sweet Shoppe, located on South Orange Avenue and 12th Street, ca. 1934.
Courtesy of the Sarandoulias Family

Postcard of the Gevas Restaurant, Gust Gevas, president, at 13 Hill Street, in the new Fatzler Building, which was adjacent to the Douglas Hotel, ca. 1930.
Courtesy of the family of Constantine and Olga Gevas

Postcard advertising Nick and Mike Mastakas's Royal Restaurant and Cocktail Lounge at 567 Broad Street, ca. 1960.
Courtesy of the Kafalas and Coniaris Families

Mr. Sarandoulias stands with friends outside his Sweet Shoppe on South Orange Avenue, ca. 1940.
Courtesy of the Sarandoulias Family

In 1930 my father owned and operated the Rialto Restaurant across from City Hall. For many years, he also was president of the National Restaurant Association.

DOT DeNICHOLAS BISBAS

My father, William, with his brother Nicholas and his brother-in-law, George Gavalas, had a restaurant called the Presto, later called the Pioneer on Market Street near Broad Street until the beginning of World War II.

EFFIE MASKALERIS VLAHAKES

Right: Mr. James Gevas, maitre d' at the Essex House, received a certificate of appreciation for his efficiency and skill in serving patrons during World War II, ca. 1944.
Courtesy of the James Gevas Family

Left: Leo Mavrades and Charles Mesenazos were partners in Scotty's Diner and Scotty's Airline Catering Company, on Highway 25, ca. 1947.
Courtesy of the Mesenazos Family

Right: Charles Kostoulakos was the bartender at the Kenmore Restaurant, ca. 1946.
Courtesy of Margaret Kostoulakos

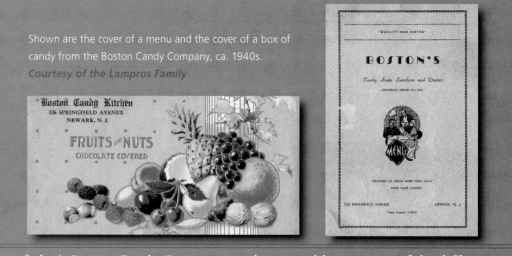

Recollections of my father's Boston Candy Company are dominated by vignettes of the different people and incidents observed over the years, rather than the physical layout of the place since all ice cream and candy stores shared physical attributes such as marble counters, booths, candy cases, scales, and wall mirrors. The quilt of personalities venturing into the place resonates with themes of joy, sadness, silliness, compassion, and frustration. Once, while eating a late lunch, a man seated at the counter managed to release a long and deeply vibrant belch as my father passed in front of him. Not missing a beat, the customer continued his meal, while my father, smiling wryly, looked at him and said, "God bless you." On one occasion, my father went into the men's restroom and found an envelope on the floor. It contained close to $1,200 in large and small bills. No identifiers were found on the envelope, so he placed it in the safe. Toward the end of the day, a rather disheartened regular customer sat at the counter lamenting the fact that he had somehow lost over a thousand dollars from his vegetable business from his truck. My father quietly asked the man to follow him to another part of the store, where he opened his safe and presented the man with the envelope, saying, "This is yours." During the summer, many neighborhood children would come in asking for water. At that time we did not have paper cups, and each glass would have to be washed by hand…water was free…dishwashers had to be paid…but the constant requests were never denied. Benevolence was not limited to children. On countless occasions, donations of various kinds were liberally shared with local indigents.

The morning after the 1967 urban disorders, my father wanted to see if anything was left of his beloved Boston Candy Company. We drove through several roadblocks where identification regarding area businessmen was checked. Upon arrival, all was well. My father and I opened the store. All who entered that day, National Guard, police, and probable looters got a chance to eat or drink in peace at that oasis known as the Boston Candy Company. It was during a lull in the day's activities that I had a chance to step outside, where I found a few people congregating. After a moment or two of chatter, I ventured a query as to my bewilderment at the fact that none of the seven large plate-glass windows had been broken. An answer came from someone in the crowd, "The old man has always been good to us." That was the essence of the Boston Candy Company.

GEORGE N. LAMPROS

Above: Michael Costopoulos, the first owner of the Boston Candy Kitchen, seated in the store with his nephew, Gus (Constantine) Nickolopoulos, and employees behind the counter, ca. 1912.
Courtesy of Michael Gionis

Left: Nicholas Lampros, in front of the display window, was the proprietor for more than fifty years of the Boston Candy Company. He bought the store from his future *koumbaro,* Michael Costopoulos, in 1924. It was located at 526 Springfield Avenue, ca. 1950.
Courtesy of the Lampros Family

Mr. Geannakakes in front of his hat-cleaning and hat-blocking establishment on West Market Street, ca. 1930.
Courtesy of Thomas Geannakakes

Left: Gus Gevas with other men at a storefront shoeshine/hat-cleaning shop. This kind of business was the gateway for thousands of teenage Greek immigrants, ca. 1920.
Courtesy of the family of Constantine and Olga Gevas

Far left: Nicholas Gianaris behind the counter of his Automatic Hat Shop at 51 West Market Street with hat blocks and blocked hats, ca. 1940s.
Courtesy of Mary G. Maroulakos

Left: Dimitri Metsopulos on his way to his shop, ca. 1930.
Courtesy of Peter J. Metsopulos

My father, Dimitri (Jim) Metsopulos, owned the Continental Hat Renovating Shop and Five Chairs Barbershop Parlor on Market and Beaver Streets. It was located just below the Paramount Theatre and Grant Lunch Cafeteria. He was well known in the Market and Broad Streets business area as the "Kaiser" because he waxed the tips of his moustache.

PETER J. METSOPULOS

Far left: Patricia Vasilion, George's daughter, by the barber pole of George's Barber Shop, located on the corner of West Market Street and High Street, September 1940.
Courtesy of Patricia Vasilion Manolis

Left: John Kehayes in front of his father's tailor business at 467 Orange Street, ca. 1920s.
Courtesy of Chrysanthy Kehayes Grieco

Mr. Petine with his four sons, Nicholas, Demetri, Mike, and George, at his shoe repair shop, located at 141 West Market Street, just before the stock market crash, ca. 1929.
Courtesy of James Petine

Father worked in Smyrna in a leather factory and gambled by buying a business [in Newark] *in the late '20s. He was strict and we worked in the store and did what he said. Papa had a hard life but always managed to put enough away for food.*

JAMES PETINE

Left: Adam A. Adams talks with Jerry Lewis and his agent, Mickey Sherman. Lewis was once an usher at the theater.
Courtesy of Adams and Pantages Families

Right: Bud Abbott, Lou Costello, their agent, and Mr. Adams in the projection room at the theater.
Courtesy of Adams and Pantages Families

While attending law school and working as a law clerk in Newark, I was still working at the Paramount Theatre, having graduated to head usher. My friends and I used to meet and walk downtown in the evening. People were always dressed. Newark was a beautiful city.

LOUIS PANTAGES

My father hired Greek Americans in his theaters to give them the chance to get an education. He would make positions, even if he did not have a job available for all Greek youth. He always invited American and Greek organizations in Newark to the theater.

Dorothea Adams Pantages

Professionals

In 1956 Doctors Antonius and Coniaris saved my life. Having gone to Long Island to bring back greens for our business, I became very ill. I ended up having chills, shakes, and a very high fever. My aunt came to bring me back to Newark. At midnight, mother called Dr. John Coniaris, who came over and immediately took me to St. Michael's Hospital, thinking I had appendicitis. The next morning, Dr. Antonius said it wasn't the appendix. My fever was at 106° F. Suddenly everyone in the family, which was strange to me, came to visit—father, sister, grandfather, including my cousin, Father Peter Kostakos. I was put in a rubber pool filled with alcohol to bring down the fever. They thought it was food poisoning. Dr. Antonius was a good doctor.

WILLIAM MAVRODE

Left: D. O. Steven A. Aridas practiced osteopathy in Newark, ca. 1940s and 1950s.
Courtesy of the Coniaris Family

Below: Reverend J. A. Aloupis and Dr. N. A. Antonius viewing the dedication plaque in the Antonius Pavilion, 1961.
Courtesy of Angelina and Nick Demas

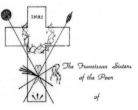

Dedication of the Antonius Pavilion Intensive Care Unit Recovery Room, February 1, 1961.
Courtesy of Angelina and Nick Demas

Dr. Peter Poulos and Dr. Charles Coniaris on
Seymour Avenue, ca. 1949.
Courtesy of the Coniaris Family

Above: *Friends, from left, Ann
Theophiles, Marika Mitilinis, Catherine
Chletsos, unknown, Pipina Valauri,
unknown, unknown, Mary Vasiliow, and
unknown meet in front of the Court
Pharmacy on West Market in Newark,
ca. 1930s.*

Left: *Mr. Pappas (Papadopoulos), the
first Greek pharmacist in Newark and
owner of the Court Pharmacy, in his
home with Mrs. Pappas, ca. 1950s.*

*Dr. Peter Poulos at Newark Babies Hospital, 15–19 Roseville Avenue, was first to practice thoracic
cardiovascular surgery on babies. He had to use a magnifying glass to find the veins.*

SPIRO POULOS

*Mr. Papadopoulos's drugstore (Court Pharmacy) was next to Dr. Antonius's office. There was a door
connecting the two, but Dr. Antonius's nurse preferred you go out the front of the doctor's office and enter
the pharmacy through its front door. There weren't any prepared, over-the-counter medicines. At the back
of the store there was a long counter, and Mr. Papadopoulos worked behind it, mixing everything by hand.
He ground the medication with a mortar and pestle and even made the tablets. He lived down near the
Essex House and took the bus every day to the pharmacy. He usually worked seven days a week, alone in
the store, from 8:00 in the morning until 10:00 at night.*

KOSTAS DIAMANDAS

"*Money was not the full measure of success; it was family and friends, living one's faith, and knowing who [you] were.*"
Corinne Pappas Maskaleris

5

Families and American Acculturation

As Greek immigrants settled in Newark, their small Greek society began to metamorphose, intermingling their homeland culture with the American way of life. Homes were becoming multilingual, sons and daughters were being educated, and young Greek Americans joined the armed forces to fight for the United States of America during World War II.

> *As children, we grew up in a secure, traditional Greek environment, a close-knit community—Greek grocery store, fish market, shoe repair, barbershop, coffeehouse, Greek school, and church activities intermingled with an American influence of diverse ethnic groups and strong patriotic fervor. There were the traditional American sports and recreational activities . . . street games, not to mention the traditional American holidays interspersed with Greek holidays. School, of course, had a great influence on the assimilation process . . . Black, Irish, Italian, German, Polish, and all Americans, each with a strong ethnic and cultural identity. In retrospect, the absence of TV was a plus.*
> ᴑ John Koronakos

The family and family life began with marriage. Fathers, brothers, relatives, or friends arranged most marriages of the first generation.

> *Proxenia (arranged marriage) was the custom and norm in Greece and in the Greek community of the early immigrants, particularly [those] from the same region.*
> ᴑ Reverend Peter Kostakos

Later, the church, various ethnic societies, and organizations provided opportunities for the succeeding generations to meet other Greek Americans with the hope that they would eventually marry within the Orthodox faith to someone of Greek descent. The welfare and unity of the Greek family took priority over any hardships they had to endure.

> *Life was hard yet simple. Family life was important. Parents worked long hours both in their businesses and at home. Sunday was the family day—attending church followed by family dinner and an afternoon outing.*
> ᴑ Stella Visas Economo

The Greek mother became the central figure in continuing the connection of the family to the Greek Orthodox faith and Hellenistic culture. Church attendance, family celebrations such as name day parties, and Greek-centered activities such as picnics and dances became her responsibility. Her influence was increasingly important in maintaining and holding on to the Greek cultural traditions with the family, as her children assimilated into the diverse fabric of the neighborhood and the American way of life.

Theodore Jovanis and Katherine Katsikas, who eventually married, were introduced at a rooftop party on Ferry Street that included family and friends. Seated in front from left: Irene, two unknown guests, and Harry. In the second row are two unknown guests, Constantine, father; Aphrodite, mother; and Katherine. Standing in back are Nick Mastakas, Theodore, and unknown. 1914.
Courtesy of the Mastakas Family

Mom lived much like the other Greek ladies of her generation, staying close to home, speaking little English, and playing hostess to my dad's friends, who were either unmarried or who had not yet brought their wives to the U.S. Our home became a center for Greeks coming to New Jersey. She was adored for her sharp wit and bottomless affection.

Tess Demas Nomos

In front of the entrance to Warren Street School are, from left, Chris Karmeris, unknown, Catherine Pulos, and Anthoula Koronakos, while in row 2 the only known student is Spiro Balatsos. In row 3 are Albert Poet, Andrew Coniaris, unknown, Louis Coviello, unknown, and Charles Coniaris, ca. 1935.
Courtesy of the Coniaris Family

I would go to Penn Station to pick up the Greek papers from New York, getting $3 a week. I needed the money for my mother. At the age of twenty-five, I wanted to buy my own business but needed $1,000. I told my mother and she gave me the money. When I asked where she got it, her answer was, "It is the money you gave me, the $3 per week which I saved for you."
    Theodore J. Bravakis

The Greek Americans celebrated many events in their lives. They observed name days (patron saints' days), usually those of the fathers, with an open house, and gave birthday and graduation parties for the children. Weddings, baptisms, anniversaries, and testimonials took place at the hotels, restaurants, halls, and community centers of the churches. Sunday dinner was also an important time for the family, since this was usually the main time a family could socialize.

Our Easter Sunday was always celebrated with the family. Our uncles, with their families, sometimes came from New York, and other times we had friends. Always with the roast leg of lamb and potatoes, spanakopita [spinach pie], Greek Easter bread, red eggs, and many other goodies.
    Margaret Apostolakos Kostoulakos

With immediate families separated by an ocean, extended families began to form within the community with friends becoming *theas* (aunts) and *theos* (uncles). Through sponsoring each other at weddings and baptisms, the *koumbari* (godparents) became second parents.

Among my memories were the aromas of our ethnic cuisine emanating from our neighbors' kitchens, the Greek music on Sunday afternoons coming from a local radio station, sitting on the front stoop of our apartment building, and greeting neighbors as they passed by, while children playing on the sidewalks were watched by their parents and grandparents. As our parents would say, it was like bringing a little part of Greece to America.
    Diana Stathopoulos

We were always in one another's houses—if they ate, you ate, in those two building, 91 and 93 West Market Street. We were like one family—the Jovanises, Juvelises, and Vlahakeses next door to the Petine's shoe repair store.
    Michael Paskas

John Kostoulakos in cap and gown for his high school graduation, ca. 1940s.
Courtesy of Toula Zanias

All the parents wanted their children to get a good education. Central High was geared for secretarial, machine shop, learning a trade, or technical courses. Many of the boys moved from Central High over to Newark College of Engineering (now NJIT). The girls went to work for the telephone company on Broad Street or the Prudential [Insurance Company] on Washington Street.
KOSTAS DIAMANDAS

117

Persifone Peters in her cheerleader outfit in front of Central High School, ca. 1945.
Courtesy of Helen Peters Cap

I went to Southside High School in Newark, making a name for myself in football. My father wanted me to quit so that I could work at the store. Since I did not know the business, I would be opening and closing the front door for $3 a week. My coach wanted me to continue playing football and gave me $5 a week to continue. This helped me get an athletic scholarship to Rollins College in Florida (all I had was a pair of sneakers). When I graduated, I returned to Newark to help my father with his import/export olive and cheese business on Clinton Place.

CHRIS A. ARGYRIS

All the children attended neighborhood public schools, among them Robert Treat, Wilson Avenue, Maple Avenue, South 10th Street, 18th Avenue, and Warren Street elementary schools. The high schools they attended included Central, East Side, West Side, South Side, Weequahic, and Arts High.

We walked to Robert Treat Elementary School, and a fine school it was. The beautiful architecture of those large arches on the exterior auditorium side, Miss Simmons playing the piano, and Mrs. Wetzel leading the morning exercises in the auditorium. We would recite the Lord's Prayer, the Pledge of Allegiance, and sing the National Anthem, then on to our studies. Central High School was also quite beautiful. The freshman initiation was to send the student to the wrong end of the fifth floor and tell them to walk across to the class they were to attend. The problem was the fifth floor had four towers and there was no way to walk across.
Ann Nikitakis Soppas

My days at West Side High School were spent in the company of students of many nationalities, races, and religions. We never thought anything of it. This was the late 1940s, early 1950s, and it was natural. No one told us we had to get along. After all, this was Newark.
Tess Demas Nomos

Even when I attended Robert Treat School in 1936, the school was integrated. My favorite friend was my black next-door neighbor. We lived on 13th Avenue across from the school.
Angeliki Skopelitis Anderson

Whether they immigrated to America or were born here, Greek was usually the children's first language. Often, school was a child's first exposure to the English language.

In September 1923, I was placed in first grade at Cleveland Public School on Bergen Avenue in Newark. Because the desks were too small—because I was fourteen years old—they brought into the classroom a large table with two chairs, and several cups and dishes with forks, knives, and spoons and a beautiful young teacher to teach me ABCs. Well, that's all I needed. I couldn't take my eyes off the teacher. But she understood how I felt and kept asking questions about the cups and the saucers. Finally, I realized that I was there to learn the English language and nothing else. I was

promoted to the seventh grade by the end of the second year. That was enough for me.
☞ Gus Janulis

In the early 1930s, the increase of Greek presence in the AFL restaurant union led to increased Greek clout in the labor movement and subsequent involvement in politics.

During the Depression, when my father lost the Gevas Restaurant, he took the Civil Service exam and came first in the state, becoming a food and drug inspector for the city of Newark. He founded the political group Greek-American Voters of Essex County. . . . He ran for district ward representative and made sure Greeks came to vote at the Hall of Records, many times cajoling or dragging them to come. Mother would make Greek goodies when he had receptions at home on Nelson Place. Many in the neighborhood, Greek, Jew, Black, and Italian, came in, and he was elected.
☞ James Gevas

My father became active in national and state Republican politics. He was Hellenic campaign manager for both Dewey and Eisenhower in the tri-state area.
☞ Loula Givas Georges

Americans of Greek descent, both men and women, served in all branches of the military and in all U.S. conflicts—World War I, World War II, the Korean War, and the Vietnam War.

Kosta Papadopoulos, the druggist's son, was in the OSS in the U.S. Army. He was captured by the Gestapo in Epirus. His Greek, the Greek he learned at the Greek school at St. Nicholas, was excellent, and his cover as a Greek native was not compromised.
☞ Reverend George A. Xenofanes

Many distinguished themselves in battle. Leonidas Gavalas graduated from Princeton University in 1934 as a lieutenant, having taken ROTC during his years there, and in 1939 chose to make the army his career. He achieved the rank of brigadier general in 1961 and major general in 1968. General Gavalas was the first American of Greek descent to reach the rank of general.

Fate played an important part in military life overseas in World War II.

I landed in Normandy during the invasion as a sergeant in combat intelligence. From a distance among the movements, I spotted a

Louis J. Bravakis of Central High School was named All City-Star Quarterback and All-State Honorable Mention, ca. 1935.
Courtesy of Theodore J. Bravakis

There were many involved in sports when I was growing up. Among the more well known: Teddy Anastos, also known as Teddy Smacka, was an outstanding boxer; the Boutsikaris brothers were famous fencers and coaches; and Louis Bravakis was an outstanding football player for Central. He died while a student and the funeral was attended by the entire student body.
PETER MEHALARIS

119

In France from left are Lt. Col. Fiche, Bing Crosby, on tour with the USO, Lt. Col. Gavalas, and an unknown soldier, August 1944.
Courtesy of George C. Pappas

Major General Leonidas George Gavalas was the first Greek American to become a general in the U.S. Army. Born April 13, 1912, in Newark and graduated from Princeton University, he entered active duty as a second lieutenant in August 1940. During World War II, he served with the First Infantry Division and with the V Corps. He was decorated by several nations for his wartime service. His American decorations include the Distinguished Service Medal, Legion of Merit, Bronze Star, and Army Commendation Medal.

COURTESY OF GEORGE C. PAPPAS

warrant officer wearing the First Infantry Division insignia. God and St. Nicholas prompted me to approach him, asking if he knew Colonel Gavalas and if he would take a note to him. My note was in Greek: "Leonide, eime etho" (Lee, I am here). I don't remember exactly how many days passed until I was told that I had been transferred to the headquarters of the first division. I cannot possibly without great emotion ably describe the feeling that I experienced when I saluted my closest friend, never imagining that I would be with him through France, Belgium, and Germany, and finally Czechoslovakia.
  Thomas A. Argyris

During World War II, while many Greek Americans served their country abroad, those who remained home sent packages and assisted the American Red Cross and Greek War Relief efforts with fundraising activities.

Mother learned only a little English because she was primarily with Greeks at home and at work. When she went to get her citizenship papers in 1944–45, the judge asked questions and she hesitated. Someone yelled out, "She's got three sons in the army, why are you questioning this lady?" She got her papers. She had three stars in her window, one for each son in the service.
  Spiro Poulos

It all began in September 1943. Fishie (Paul Buclary) and I went marching down West Market Street while our mothers tearfully watched from the window of our apartment. We were ordered to report to the post office in downtown Newark. Again, tears as we marched past my father's restaurant. He and the waitresses were waving goodbye as we marched to Penn Station. Little did our parents realize how glad we were to be leaving. Both Paul and I had older brothers in service, so it's understandable why our parents would feel apprehensive.
  Peter Jovanis

Additionally, the endeavors of many of the Greek American organizations, such as GAPA and AHEPA, supported the United States of America by raising funds for war bonds and the American Red Cross while also supporting the Greek War Relief effort.

In December 1946, Hellenic Post 440 was established to honor the men of Hellenic descent who made the supreme sacrifice in World Wars I and II.

This official photograph of Major General Leonidas Gavalas, fourth U.S. Army Chief of
Staff, at Fort Sam Houston, Texas, was taken in June 1969.
Courtesy of George N. Lampros

It officially joined the ranks of the American Legion on March 22, 1947. The post is
dedicated to the welfare of its members, contributing to the overall community and
to the United States of America.

Many of the returning servicemen continued their service to their communities.
Tony Genakos became an FBI agent, and Gus Theodos and Peter Thomas joined
the Newark Police Department.

Photos on both pages: Greek Independence Day Parade members of Hellenic Post 440 American Legion in Evzone costumes assembling before and marching in a parade, on Broad Street, ca. 1947. *Courtesy of the Coniaris Family, Dessa Halakos Weiss, and Hellenic Post 440, American Legion*

After his discharge from the Navy, Peter Thomas went to Bloomfield College and received his BA degree. He took the police exam and became a patrolman in the Newark Police Department. Peter worked in the First Precinct and had the reputation of having cleaned up Mulberry Street singlehandedly. In 1970 Peter was shot while escorting the manager of the Acme to the bank. Fortunately, he survived, but still has a bullet somewhere in the back of his head/neck, which did not penetrate the skull. After the shooting, Peter worked as Judge Hazelwood's aide in the courts.

 Mary Thomas Marolakos

The Greek ethic has always been to work hard and to become involved—with one's family, friends, neighbors, community, and country.

Today most of my closest friends have moved on and out of the area, but we still see each other and talk about the good days. We exposed the Greek people to the rest of the community. We showed how hardships were overcome by our parents, how they made something of themselves, and in a sense, if you were wise enough, you carried on those traditions with your children. Everything taught to me by my mother, father, and mother-in-law has been passed on to my children and grandchildren.

Dr. Charles Coniaris

Weddings

Catherine Theofilopoulou and Christos Galanopoulos photographed at their wedding on May 22, 1911.
Courtesy of Helen Galanoplos

Wedding invitation of Catherine Theofilopoulou and Christos Galanopoulos.

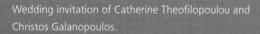

Yianoula and Nikita Juvelis on September 6, 1913.
Courtesy of the Juvelis Family

124

Mr. and Mrs. Peter
Linardakis, ca. 1922.
*Courtesy of the
Linardakis Family*

Wedding of Mr. and Mrs. Sam Coniaris, January 1922.
Courtesy of Coniaris Family

Left: Peter and Mary
Koronakos, ca. 1919.
Courtesy of John Koronakos

Right: The wedding of Mr.
and Mrs. William Pallantios,
ca. 1923.
*Courtesy of James
Pallantios*

*We grew up in the same community, went to school together, also Greek School and St. Nicholas Church.
We knew each other since childhood. We got married in 1959.*

JOHN AND VIRGINIA (PILAVAKIS) TSAPTSINOS

George Visas and Sophia Sousanis, ca. 1916.
Courtesy of the Economo Family

Mr. and Mrs. John Nikitakis, ca. 1925.
Courtesy of Ann Nikitakis Soppas

Marie Johnson and Adam A. Adams
(Adamopoulos), August 17, 1917.
*Courtesy of the Adams
and Pantages Families*

Sam and Anna Markos, ca. 1931.
Courtesy of the Sam Markos Family

Peter Thomas and Kaliope Demetroulakos, ca. 1932.
Courtesy of Mary Thomas Marolakos

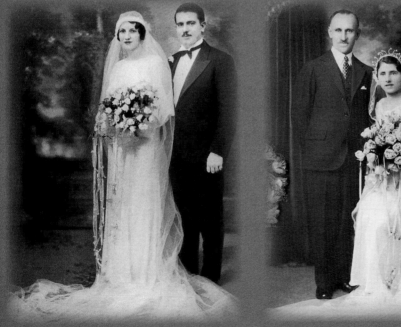

Anna and Chris Sarandoulias, ca. 1934.
Courtesy of the Sarandoulias Family

Nicholas and Vassiliki Lampros, June 20, 1935.
Courtesy of the Lampros Family

The wedding of Asimina Blikas and Athanasios Zois with, from left: Toula Speros, Bertha Pallantios, unknown, Athanasios Anagnostis, *koumabaros*, Athanasios Blikas, Chris Gavalas, unknown, Fautini Zois, and Stamatia Zois, January 24, 1937.
Courtesy of the Athanasios Zois Family

Angelica George and George Lymp (Lymperopoulos), ca. 1937.
Courtesy of Mrs. Joseph Woznicki

Wedding reception of George Argyris and Mary (Kambissis) Argyris on November 23, 1919, at Washington Hall, Newark.
Courtesy of Esther Argyris Chrisicos

Wedding reception of Stephan Argyriou and Sophia (Papastathi) Argyriou, August 28, 1921.
Courtesy of Esther Argyris Chrisicos

The wedding party includes, from left: Chris Sarames, Bertha (Pallantios) Sarames, James Pallantios, Harriet (Dillon), and Peter Pallantios (bride and groom), Mrs. Christina Pallantios, Mr. and Mrs. Peter J. Curtis, ca. 1949.
Courtesy of James Pallantios

Left: Thomas and Katherine Gecas with their *koumbari*, ca. 1920s.
Courtesy of Bessie Kostins Mamalou

129

Celebrating the marriage of Connie and Tony Vlahakes at the end of World War II with some of the bridal party still in uniform, from left: Tom Geannakakes, Ethel Juvelis, John Vlahakes, Connie Geannakakes, Tony Vlahakes, Ellie Moukas, Peter Vlahakes, Bertha Pallantios, and Tula Geannakakes. June 17, 1945.
Courtesy of the Vlahakes Family

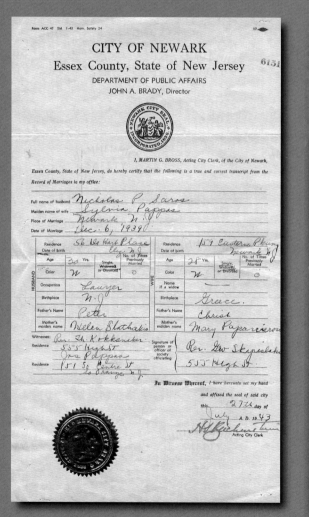

Certificate of marriage issued by the City of Newark to Nicholas P. Saros and Sylvia Pappas, 1943.
Courtesy of Ileana N. Saros

Jerry Economo and Stella (Visas) Economo with the *koumbaro* George Kyriakoulias, ring bearer John Barlas, and maid of honor Helen Visas. August 25, 1946.
Courtesy of the Economo Family

Above: The Chris Vasiliow wedding party, from left: John Gianas, Helen Gianas Patsis, Chris and Mary Gianas Vasiliow, Catherine Gianas Kassel, and Thomas A. Argyris. May 1949.
Courtesy of the Gianas Vasilow Family

Below: The Kostas Diamandas wedding party, ca. 1953—seated from left: Bess Kostins, Nia Christman, Pamela Kostoulakos, Diane Stathopoulos, Fran Gallos; standing from left: James Gevas, Nick Juvelis, Steve Diamandas, Estelle Bravakis, Mary and Kostas Diamandas, Anthony Diamandas, James Nikitakis, and Aristo Koutoukidis.
Courtesy of the Diamandas Family

Wedding photo, ca. 1950s. In the back from left: are John Padakis, *koumbaro*, Nicholas and Ethel Frankos, Zenovia Padakis; in the front from the left are Asemina Padakis Hintze, Theona Padakis Paleologos, and Peter Padakis.
Courtesy of Ona Frankos Spiridellis

Everyone in the Greek community of Newark was often invited to wedding receptions. More men than women attended because originally, men had immigrated from Greece to the United States with the women arriving as brides after World War I.

Families

The Costopoulos Family, ca. 1911, seated from left: Constantine Nickolopoulos, next to his father, Themistocles Nickolopoulos, Angeliki Costopoulos, Panagiotis Arianas. Standing from left: Olympia Costopoulos, Stamatike Nickolopoulos, Demosthenis Costopoulos, Michael Costopoulos, Eleni Arianas, and Politimi Costopoulos.
Courtesy of Paul (Papandreopoulos) Andrews and Perry P. Zagoreos

Metsopulos Family, ca. 1920s, seated from left: Gus Mantzaris, Peter Metsopulos's godfather, and his mother, Eugenia Metsopulos; standing from left are Peter, Charles, and Helen Metsopulos.
Courtesy of Peter J. Metsopulos

Mr. and Mrs. George Kafalas with baby
Steve, ca. 1915.
Courtesy of the Kafalas Family

Constantine wearing a World War I uniform,
Themistocles, and Angeliki Nickopoulos wearing
a Red Cross outfit, ca. 1918.
Courtesy of Paul (Papandreopoulos) Andrews

Left: The Pappas (Papachristou) Family, ca. 1920.
In back row from left: Peter, Tom, George, and
John Kafalas. Front row: Christine; Mrs. Pappas;
Sylvia; Penelope, John's wife, with the Kafalas
children.
Courtesy of Ileana N. Saros

Newark was a small enough city that everyone was close to each other. Though I grew up being a normal American kid, I was also expected to be aware of my Greek heritage. I got a nickel to go to the corner to get a Fudgesicle, cut up my skates to make a scooter out of orange crates, played with tops, marbles, and flipped cards. On weekends, we usually had dinner at one of our relatives' homes. We spoke only Greek at home and we ate only traditional Greek food. I had no idea about grilled cheese, meatloaf, or hot dogs. We ate pastitsio *[baked noodles],* spanakopita *[spinach pie], and* keftedes *[meatballs].*

I learned that in America you can accomplish whatever you wish. Only you can put a restriction on yourself. I had the best mentors—commitment from my grandfather, moral strength from my father, and the love of history and the arts from my uncle.

PAUL (PAPANDREOPOULOS) ANDREWS

Above left: Mr. and Mrs. Bacchus and daughters Helen on left and Katina on right, ca. 1920s.
Courtesy of Calomria Papageorge Canaris

Above right: Nicholas Evrotas and son, June 23, 1921.
Courtesy of Calomira Papageorge Canaris

Eugenia and Nicholas Faraklas with their children Ted, Mary, and Sylvia, ca. 1929.
Courtesy of the Faraklas Family

John George Bravakis, with his six children, ca. 1920, assumed the responsibility of his deceased brother's five children. First row seated from left: Sophie J., Martha P., and Louis J. Second row: George P., Kathryn J., John Bravakis with Ida P. on his lap, Theodore J., Lillian P., and Louis P., while standing in back are George J. and Stella J.
Courtesy of Theodore John Bravakis

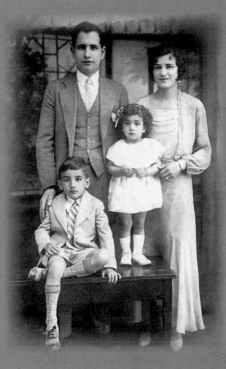

Nick and Euterpe Diamandas with sons Kostas and Steve, 1933.
Courtesy of the Diamandas Family

Mr. and Mrs. Nikitakis with son, Jim, and daughter, Ann, ca. 1931.
Courtesy of the Nikitakis Family

Panagiota Gellas holding George, ca. 1930s, with her other children standing. From left: Florence, Gus, Jim, and Joanna.
Courtesy of the Gellas Family

Left: The Tsotakos family, from left: Georgia, Stella, and Pauline Tsotakos with Anthony Panagakos and Michael Pontiakos in front, ca. 1930s.
Courtesy of Mary Thomas Marolakos

The Adams family includes from left: Adam, Thomas, Marie, Emanuel, Dorothea, and Peter, photographed in their home on Chancellor Avenue, ca. 1930s.
Courtesy of the Adams and Pantages Families

Nicholas and Margaret Bistis are holding their son, Matthew, ca. 1920s.
Courtesy of the Bistis Family

Iphegenia and Spyridon Basil Kehayes with their son, Basil, ca. 1930s.
Courtesy of Chrysanthy Kehayes Grieco

136

The Koronakos family ca. 1930—father Panagioti and grandmother Stavroula with, from left, front row, John, Chris, and Toula; back, Stella, Anna, and Fota.
Courtesy of the Koronakos Family

Anna Markos holding son, Peter, on her lap with Irene Pavlakos and Antoinette Markos, ca. 1939.
Courtesy of the Sam Markos Family

The Pallantios Families, ca. 1930s.
Courtesy of James Pallantios

Antonia and John Kostakos with their children, ca. 1940s—standing from left are Georgia, Lula, Steve, and Charles.
Courtesy of Charles Kostakos

The family of Christos and Catherine Galanopoulos, ca. 1930s, includes their children, from left, Eugenia; Ruth; on lap, John; Anastasios; and George.
Courtesy of Helen Galanoplos

James and Rebecca Nicholas Family, ca. 1950. Seated is James, and standing from left are Constance, Rebecca, and Eugenia.
Courtesy of Constance Nicholas Krentz

The William Zois Family, ca. 1939—seated from left are Harry, Penny, and Nick, while standing are Stamatia; William, father; Chrysoula, mother; Gus, and Katherine.
Courtesy of the Athanasios Zois Family

The Soterios Corodemus Family—standing from left are Helen Corodemus Loukedis, Soterios Corodemus, Marina Corodemus; seated from left are James Corodemus, Stella Corodemus Bales, Christy Corodemus, ca. 1936.
Courtesy of the Corodemus Family

Helen and Paul Katsamakis with sons, John and Anthony Vlastaras, ca. 1935.
Courtesy of the Sarandoulias Family

Michael Poulos, center, patriarch of the family, pictured with Frank, Mollie, and John on the right. Chris with Ourania, Alice, and Betty are on the left, 1940.
Courtesy of John F. Poulos

The Gargas Family in May 1931—bottom, from left: George, father Anastasios, Stephanos Mimides, mother Athanasia, and Michael; in back, from left: John, Anita Mimides, and Panagioti.
Courtesy of George A. Gargas

Above left: The Argyris brothers. Seated from left are Stephen, Archie, and George. Standing are Tom and John, ca. 1920s.
Courtesy of Esther Argyris Chrisicos

Above right: John Jolas is holding Mary, and Mrs. Stella Jolas with the twins, Constantine and Pauline, ca. 1933.
Courtesy of the Jolas Family

Left: Presbytera Georgia Aloupis and daughter, Constance, after they first arrived in Newark when Reverend James A. Aloupis became pastor of St. Nicholas Greek Orthodox Church, ca. 1954.
Courtesy of Gus Theodos

Children

This is Antonia Mehalaris' official City of Newark certificate and record of birth.
Courtesy of Peter Mehalaris

Brother and sister George and Kikitsa Georgopoulos
Georges, ca. 1920s.
Courtesy of the Georgopoulos Family

Steve and Constantine Maskaleris, ca. 1920s.
Courtesy of Corinne Pappas Maskaleris

Sisters Demi and Kiki Lampros, ca. 1939.
Courtesy of the Lampros Family

Theodore J. Bravakis, wearing his AHEPA fez, stands next to his sister, Katherine Bravakis, ca. 1920s.
Courtesy of Mary Thomas Marolakos

George N. Lampros at three years of age, 1946.
Courtesy of the Lampros Family

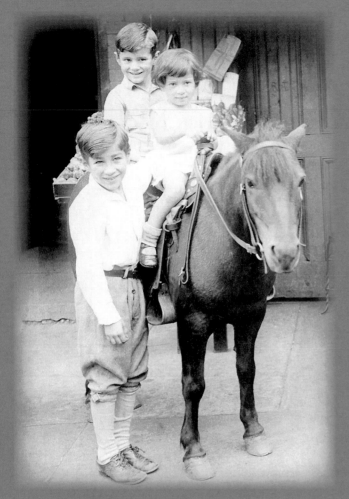

Kafalas children Betty and John on pony, with James holding the reigns, ca. 1931.
Courtesy of the Kafalas and Coniaris Families

Baby John Lollos, ca. 1939.
Courtesy of John Lollos

Peter, Helen, and Percy Peters (Petropoulos), ca. 1938.
Courtesy of Helen Peters Cap

Ona and Steven Frankos, ca. 1944.
Courtesy of Ona Frankos Spiridellis

Marigo and Corinne Pappas, ca. 1937.
Courtesy of Corinne Pappas Maskaleris

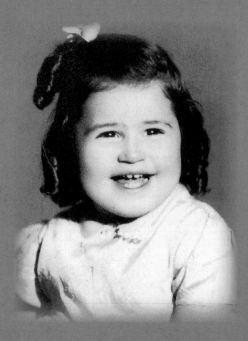

Ann Costopoulos, ca. 1946.
Courtesy of Paul (Papandreopoulos) Andrews

Left: Dressed for Easter Sunday are the Juvelis children—from top left, Ethel, Nick, Angelina; from bottom left, George, Stelio, and Helen, April 1936.
Courtesy of the Juvelis Family

Celebrations

John Poutsiaka posing for his high
school graduation, ca. 1920s.
Courtesy of John Poutsiaka

At the Essex Hotel wedding reception, Constantine Pappas and Georgia Gavalas Pappas are standing, while seated from left are her mother,
Dena Gavalas; Archbishop Athenagoras, later becoming Patriarch in Constantinople; Reverend George Spyridakis; and her father, George Gavalas,
February 1940.
Courtesy of George C. Pappas

After Sunday dinner at the Petine home, the family gather outside with, back right, John, the tailor; Charles Mistra, a bachelor who never missed a Sunday meal; and a young girl staying with the family for a while, ca. 1930s.
Courtesy of James Petine

Celebrating Easter on Bank Street are first row from left: Gus Matzaris, unknown, Dimitri, Nicholas, and Eugenia Metsopulos, Tini, Martha, and Nicholas Gianaris holding Katherine. Second row: Panagiotis Kaplanes holding Helen Metsopulos, Theophanes Lemberes holding Charles Metsopulos, Georgia Gianaris held by unknown member, and Sarantos Stathopoulos, ca. 1921.
Courtesy of the Metsopulos Family

In keeping with the Easter traditions from Greece, my family would roast a whole lamb over an open fire by turning the spit by hand. The lamb was prepared the night before. The charcoal fire was started early in the morning. We all took turns. Neighbors would stop by, taking a turn at the spit while joining us in a glass of wine and an appetizer.

PETER J. METSOPULOS

Relatives and friends attend the annual name day open house held in honor of Constantine "Gus" Gevas standing at the head of the table, with Olga Gevas and Reverend Spyridakis in the front, ca. 1940s.
Courtesy of the family of Constantine and Olga Gevas

Four generations celebrate the fiftieth wedding anniversary of Mr. and Mrs. Kallianis, ca. 1950s.
Courtesy of Reverend George A. Xenofanes

Our home was open house for Father's name day. You did not invite people; they just knew it was open house at George the barber's house.
PATRICIA VASILION MANOLIS

Above: Mr. Peter Thomas, third from left, of St. Demetrios at his testimonial dinner for his service as president of the Board of Trustees. With Mr. Thomas, from left, are Reverend Spyridakis, Mrs. Thomas, and Reverend Papademetriou, ca. 1950s.
Courtesy of Helen Thomas Roy

Below: On December 3, 1944, family and friends gather at the Sheraton Hotel to celebrate the christening of George Lampros. The photograph and list of guests appeared in the New York Greek newspaper *Atlantis* under the heading "Greeks in America," written by Mr. Dermousis, the social editor for Newark.
Courtesy of the Lampros Family

Mrs. Dermousis, a Greek language tutor named Mother of the Year, receives a bouquet of flowers on Mother's Day, ca. 1940s.
Courtesy of Tom Demery

St. Dionisos day fell on December 17. We made kourambiedes *[nut shortbread cookies] and sometimes* diples *[fried honey pastry]. In the early years, we would dance and have a great time with friends and relatives.*

Margaret Apostolakos Kostoulakos

Politics

Governor Robert Meyner with Reverends Coutros, Condoleon, and Aloupis with John Thevos and Charles Mesenazos seated to the right of the governor in the governor's office, ca. 1950s.
Courtesy of Nicholas Chatzopoulos

On October 29, 1944, the United Greek American Voters League held a dance celebrating the liberation of Greece and the reelection of President Roosevelt at the Continental Ballroom on Broad Street. The speaker is the league president, Constantine (Gus) Gevas. The U.S. Marine at the microphone is John Linardakis, who saw combat at Iwo Jima and Guadalcanal.
Courtesy of the family of Constantine and Olga Gevas

My father, Spiredon Apostolos Vardakis, who had an appreciation of history and a love for the written word, visited the Freedom Train when it came to Newark in 1947. The Freedom Train, sponsored by the American Heritage Foundation, carried on board an exhibit of priceless original documents proclaiming principles of freedom, such as the Federalist Papers, the Declaration of Independence, the Constitution, and the Magna Carta. The train brought the exhibit to towns and cities in each state. "Our American Heritage," a collection of copies of the original documents in the exhibit, published by the American Heritage Foundation, was offered to the visiting public. Father kept this collection on his desk with his dictionaries.

ARTEMIS VARDAKIS

Governor Meyner at left, with Michael Gargas; Archbishop Iakovos, Primate of the Greek Orthodox Church of North and South America; Charles Mesenazos; and William Chirgotis, ca. 1950s.
Courtesy of the Mesenazos Family

USO letter of appreciation to Mrs. Asimina (Minnie) Zois, January 20, 1967.
Courtesy of the Athanasios Zois Family

Diana Stathopoulos, Athena Gougoumis, unknown, Demi Lampros, unknown, unknown, Freda Katramados, and Mary T. Marolakos preparing a mailing for the campaign, ca. 1968.
Courtesy of the Lampros Family

The U.S. Post Office, Newark, New Jersey, honored Mrs. Asimina (Minnie) Zois in the 1960s for twenty-five years of sending packages to American and Greek American servicemen as well as underprivileged people in Greece.

Military

Medal with ribbons of Thomas Gecas, World War I.
Courtesy of Bessie Kostins Mamalou

Officer Peter Metsopulos received the Silver Star for covering a concussion-type grenade with his steel helmet, preventing greater injuries to his comrades. The four Metsopulos brothers served their country in World War II. Three of the Metsopulos brothers were wounded in combat during their tours of duty in Europe, ca. 1940s.
Courtesy of the Metsopulos Family

Thomas Gecas, seated, served four tours of duty during World War I, including the battles of San Mihiel and Meuse Argonne.
Courtesy of Bessie Kostins Mamalou

My uncle, Thomas Gecas, was gassed in World War I and died later from complications. I was about ten years old and I remember him in bed, unable to eat because of cancer of the throat.
BESSIE KOSTINS MAMOLOU

Gold Stars have been a symbol of loss since World War I. Families hung service banners in their windows with blue stars for each member serving in the armed forces. If one was killed in action, the blue star was covered with a gold one.

Anna Koronakos had the rank of first class storekeeper in the WAAVs (Women's Naval Auxiliary Corps) and was stationed in Annapolis. At the same time, her sister, Fota, was in the WAACs (Women's Auxiliary Army Corps).
Courtesy of John Koronakos

Patricia Vasilion of 36 West Market Street, cashier at several Newark theaters, enlisted in the WAACs. At a flag-raising ceremony at South Orange and Springfield Avenues, she addressed the crowds and sold $3,100 in war bonds, October 18, 1943.
COURTESY OF PATRICIA VASILION MANOLIS

At the time of the first World War, my father and my uncle enlisted in the Army, my father being sent to Panama, my uncle to France. Upon discharge in 1918, they were both awarded citizenship. My father, proud of his service in the American armed forces in World War I, was very much involved with the American Legion.
JOHN KORONAKOS

Brothers John Koronakos, above, in the U.S. Navy in 1947, and Chris Koronakos, right, at age eighteen, in training for the Air Force in 1946.
Courtesy of John Koronakos and Marion Koronakos

Left: Captain, U.S. Air Force, Peter L. Vlahakes was a navigator on B24 bombers, ca. 1944.
Courtesy of Peter L. Vlahakes

Brothers Nick and Bill flank their mother, Cleopatra Katsulakos. Both served in the Navy, ca. 1944.
Courtesy of the Lampros Family

I was awarded the Air Medal and Silver Star for gallantry in action. Our plane, B-24, on which I was a navigator, raided the seaport of Pylos in Greece, which the Germans were using to send war supplies to the North African–German Army.

PETER L. VLAHAKES

Charles Karakos sits in his jeep while serving in Europe during World War II, ca. 1940.
Courtesy of the Lampros Family

Army Captain Louis J. Pantages served in World War II in England, France, Belgium, and Germany and was part of the Normandy invasion, landing at Omaha Beach, ca. 1940.
Courtesy of the Adams and Pantages Families

Seaman Peter Kostoulakos, ca. 1940s.
Courtesy of the Kostoulakos Family

My brother served as an enlisted man in the Navy during World War II and was an officer in the Army during the Korean War.
LOULA GIVAS GEORGES

Charles Kostoulakos, ca. 1940s.
Courtesy of the Kostoulakos Family

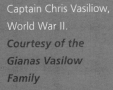
Captain Chris Vasilow, World War II.
Courtesy of the Gianas Vasilow Family

Paul Kostoulakos, ca. 1940s.
Courtesy of Tula Zanias

Mr. and Mrs. Dan Kostoulakos of 142 Warren Street had four sons in the service in World War II—John, fighting in the Pacific; Peter, aboard the USS Oklahoma; Charles, a prisoner in Germany; and Paul, stationed at Fort Dix, ca. 1940s.

COURTESY OF THE KOSTOULAKOS FAMILY

Discipline was very strict at the Naval Training Station in Newport, Rhode Island. You were taught to salute anyone who even looked like an officer. I once saluted the Coca-Cola man.

PETER JOVANIS

Above: Sylvia and Nicholas Saros before he left to serve in the Army. Nicholas was in both the European and Pacific Theaters of Operation, while Sylvia worked as a legal secretary in Newark, ca. 1940s.
Courtesy of Ileana N. Saros

Right: Gus George, pictured here in 1936, achieved the rank of lieutenant colonel, assistant inspector general of First Army, and received the First Army Certificate of Achievement from Brig. Gen. C. R. Hutchison, deputy chief of staff of First Army, on November 30, 1954.
Courtesy of the Woznicki Family

The four sons of Reverend Nicholas Triandafilou all served in the armed services during World War II— the three older ones in the Air Force and the youngest as a Marine officer who was involved in the battle of Iwo Jima. During the latter part of the war, the oldest son, Charles, was involved in a plane accident and died from his injuries. The second oldest served as an aerial photographer for close to four years, receiving a leg injury during that time. The third son, Angelo, was a B-24 pilot and after twenty missions over Okinawa crashed on the way to his base. He lost his life two weeks before V-J Day. A son was born to his wife a month later.

LOUIS TRIANDAFILOU

War Relief

Right: Receipt for dues to the Newark Chapter of the American National Red Cross and a ribbon worn to support the Greek War Relief effort, ca. 1940s.
Courtesy of George C. Pappas

Below: Reverend George Spyridakis, Adam A. Adams, his daughter, Dorothea, and son, Peter, standing in front of the Adams Theatre as people line up for the Special War Bond Premiere of *Going My Way,* ca. 1940s.
Courtesy of the Adams and Pantages Families

Above: Women of the Greek American community gathered in a Bradford Place storefront to support, through a knitting project, the American war effort and the Greek War Relief, ca. 1940. *Courtesy of the Phillips Family*

Right: Supporting the activities of the American Red Cross during World War II are: row 1 from left, Mrs. Vasiliow, Mrs. Chiminides and unknown; row 2: Mrs. Kanas, Mrs. Costopoulos, Mrs. Scorda, and Mrs. De Nicholas, ca. 1940s. *Courtesy of Mary Pantelis, Pipina Valauri, Louise Vasiliow*

Adam A. Adams had hired the Andrews Sisters and Artie Shaw and his band to perform at a Greek War Relief event. When the entertainers finished and were on their way out, a Greek band came on, and as the clarinetist started, Artie Shaw heard the sound, spun around, and stayed to listen.

JOANNA GELLAS

Left: Reverend George Spyridakis, Mr. Steve Gevas, Ambassador Lellis of Greece, Archbishop Athenagoras, Dr. Nicholas Antonius, Mr. Adam A. Adams, and Mr. Harold J. Adonis attend a fundraising event for the Greek War Relief, ca. 1940s. *Courtesy of the Adams and Pantages Families*

Below: At a reception in Newark, Ambassador Lellis joins the Greek American mothers whose sons are in the armed forces of the United States, ca. 1940s. *Courtesy of the Adams and Pantages Families*

Above: Women in regional Greek costumes dance at a fundraising event for the Greek War Relief Association. From left: Mary Vasiliow, Helen Aridas, Pauline Tsotakos, and Sophie Paskas, ca. 1940s.
Courtesy of Mary Pantelis, Pipina Valauri, Louise Vasiliow

Right: Cleopatra Katsulakos is dressed in Greek regional attire collecting funds for the Greek War Relief on Broad Street, ca. 1940s.
Courtesy of the Lampros Family

Above: Katherine Gevas Botsolas dressed as Miss America and Katina Kallianis dressed as Miss Greece ready to join the Greek American parade on Broad Street, ca. 1942.
Courtesy of Eugenia Gevas Fadil

Left: Ann Nickopoulos in an Amalia costume preparing to collect funds for the Greek War Relief effort, ca. 1940s.
Courtesy of Paul (Papandreopoulos) Andrews

A float of the Parthenon with young women dressed in classical Greek costumes celebrating the Greek American parade on Broad Street, August 15, 1942.
Courtesy of John Lollos

"*The Greek-American presence in the city lasted one hundred years. They found work, built churches, started businesses, educated their children, celebrated their culture, fought our wars, and then were gone, migrating elsewhere in New Jersey and other states. It was the American dream fulfilled.*"
Charles F. Cummings, Newark City Historian

6

More Voices and Images

The Newark immigrant experience is a microcosm of other diverse ethnic groups in the United States. Their stories are all of our stories; their voices are all of our voices. Their willingness to make sacrifices, to improve their status economically and socially, and to educate their children was their challenge and their legacy. Adjusting to a new land had its hardships, yet no matter where the Greeks landed, they survived and they remembered.

As a child, I often accompanied my grandfather on his walks. He carried a cane because of a disability. I was about as tall as his cane when we would walk our neighborhood in Newark. We usually wound up in West Side Park, where he taught me to pitch stones. Now, as an adult, when I need to ponder an issue, I take his cane with me for a walk. It makes me feel as if he is with me. I can visualize us walking down Springfield Avenue again.
Paul (Papandreopoulos) Andrews

My father fought in the Battle of Verdun in 1917 in World War I so he could become an American citizen. The focus of our life was to assimilate, be American, be proud to be an American, and be proud of our Greek heritage. My father was very Americanized, never spoke Greek in the store. He even had a fifteen-foot oil painting commissioned of George Washington crossing the Delaware—because he was the Father of our Country—hanging in the store.
John Lollos

Our formative years were centered around the church, Greek School, and social, interrelated activities. We formed theatrical groups and wrote, directed, and acted in Greek and American plays presented primarily for the Greek community.
Thomas A. Argyris

Most of the Saint Nicholas dances were held at the Essex House Hotel on Broad Street, attracting several thousand people. The bar was four deep, and the Continental Ballroom, where I saw Sophia Vembo (a famous singer from Greece who was the voice of encouragement for the Greeks during World War II) give an unforgettable performance in 1946.
John F. Poulos

Our church dance was an event to behold, formal and elegant. Some of the sites of the event were the Robert Treat Hotel, the Mosque, Continental Ballroom, and the Essex House.
Ann Nikitakis Soppas

When the church had dances, Mr. Criona would translate American songs with Greek words. I particularly remember a Greek version of "Besame Mucho."
Mary Faraklas Diamandas

Angeliki and Elias with their son, Politimos, on Springfield Avenue, ca. 1940s.
Courtesy of Paul (Papandreopoulos) Andrews

In the 1920s, my father, John, worked for one of the bread companies in Newark, delivering bread by horse and wagon. He later opened a small coffeehouse on Warren Street near Lock Street, which he lost during the Depression. Pota, my mother, went to work in a cigar factory for a while when they first came to Newark. In 1933 Pota got a job in the Clark Thread Company.

⁓ Mary Thomas Marolakos

Since Newark was the center for leather, my father began working in a leather factory on Frelinghuysen Avenue. He walked to work because he didn't have the 5 cents for the bus. Then he opened the first food market, the Paramount, at 212 Academy Street. I would work there after school and on weekends. In 1924, after Tom and I were married, he took over the business from my father, which was now on West Market Street. We were in business for thirty-two years, twenty-five of them with my husband. Throughout the years, we hired helpers from the Greek community.

⁓ Bertha Pallantios Manos

Members of the St. Demetrios Greek Orthodox Drama Group after a performance of a Greek play with Greek School teacher Mrs. Psihas on the right and Mr. Thomas, president of the community, on the left, ca. 1940s.
Courtesy of the Kafalas and Coniaris Families

In 1938 my father, John, was unloading greens on New Street. Edward Arnold, a banker, (deals done with handshake) came down the street, where he had foreclosed on a building. "John, why don't you buy this building? I want you to have it for $1,000.

The Essex House.
Courtesy of The Newark Public Library

The Hotel Douglas, the Military Park Hotel, and the Essex House were the sites of many social and fundraising dinner dances for the Greek churches and social organizations as well as family celebrations.

Top: The Hotel Douglas.
Courtesy of The Newark Public Library

Bottom: The Military Park Hotel, demolished in 1993.
Courtesy of The Newark Public Library

Whatever you can pay me each month." So he [my father] moved from 19th Street, rented a house and garages, and moved to New Street. He stayed there, became a florist, and we had a thriving business.
— William Mavrode

Dad was first chef at the South Park Restaurant. On the day of his wedding, June 16, 1925, he went to work in the morning and cooked the food for the reception. Feeling prepared, he then went to his wedding, which was performed by Father Spyridakis at 220 Academy Street.
— Ann Nikitakis Soppas

We lived on Chancellor Avenue, and Mother would put us on the bus and give us 5 cents to go to downtown Newark. Father's secretary would pick us up, take us to lunch, and then to our father's movie theater to see a movie. People would go to movies with white gloves, all dressed up. Newark was a lovely area.
— Dorothea Adams Pantages

My father bought my brother and me two Nider shoeshine chairs. All the money, including tips, went into a tin bank for school and to buy clothes. Every Saturday night he gave us a nickel to go across the street and buy candy. Every other week we would go to the Court Theater. After Sunday dinner, he would go to bed for two to three hours to sleep. We played lotto around the kitchen table until he woke up, and then Papa and Mama went to the movies.
— James Petine

My grandfather changed his last name to Nicholas from Nicolaou so he would be recognized as an American. After gaining his citizenship papers, he and my grandmother, Anna, opened the City Restaurant in Newark. They purchased a small home on Arch Street where my mother, Helen Nicholas Theodos, was born in 1912. My mother attended East Side High School and upon completion, she was matched with my father, Nicholas Theodosopoulos.
— Gus Theodos

For the first thirty years of my life, I lived on West Market Street. Everything we needed was within walking distance. This was my world. Few of us had cars, we seldom rode on the buses, and only in an emergency took a taxicab. We walked to our church, to our schools, to the hospital, to the grocery stores, to drugstores, the

department stores, the candy and ice cream shops, the theaters, the library, and best of all, to Branch Brook Park.
  Mary G. Maroulakos

A journey down West Market Street included buying Greek and American products at the Paramount Food Store operated by Tom and Bertha Manos, getting a haircut at Mr. Staikos's barbershop, going to Dr. Antonius for physicals, leaving via the Papadopoulos Drug Store for prescriptions, and buying a radio made up of different parts from the Atlas Radio store owned by Charles Verginis (the war prevented new radios being made). Going on to Plane Street, eating lunch at Thomas's Greek restaurant serving only Greek food and pastry; a wonderful memory of the delicious food and friendly service of the Greek waiters. Heading downtown was Mr. Dermousis's store selling the Greek papers daily, stefana *[wedding wreaths],* kandelia *[candles], baptism outfits, and Greek records, which you could listen to before purchasing. Across the street was the Kapetanakos Photo Studio above the 5 & 10 cent store, and on the lower lobby he had placed pictures of many Greek families and weddings. On Broad Street was the Argyris Shoe Repair shop (repairs "while you wait"), the Matthews Coffee shop next to the Newsreel Theatre, and the Central Restaurant, near Raymond Boulevard with all Greek workers and owners.*
  John F. Poulos

West Market Street was the central area of Greek Town. The West End was Norfolk Street near where I lived with my parents, Arthur (Athanasios) and Rita (Rigoula), and brother, Louis (Elias), in a coldwater railroad flat over a candy store and luncheonette. Above us on the next floor lived Nicholas and Lambrini Migakis. My father and Nicholas loved each other as neighbors and as good friends, and each made wine every year, keeping it in their own cellar compartment secured with three to four locks each. That was as far as their neighborly love would go.
  Reverend George A. Xenofanes

I was very fortunate to live in a neighborhood that had a large Greek populace. I lived in an eight-family house, and seven of the eight families were Greek. The owner, who lived on the second floor, was the only non-Greek; he was Italian. The neighborhood may be gone, but many of the friends from those days are still in my life today.
  Charles J. Kostakos

Catherine Karakos and her cousin, James Kiriakarakos, on Stirling Street, ca. 1934.
Courtesy of the Lampros Family

My father, who was born in Turkey, emigrated to Kalamata, Peloponnesos, Greece with his mother after the Turks killed his father. That is where my parents met and married. My mother, who was born in the U.S. and went to live in Kalamata, Peloponnesos, at the age of three, had to return to the U.S. to renew her citizenship. We came to Newark in 1955. Both my parents had to work. As the oldest child in my family, I was like a young mother taking care of my younger sisters and brother.
Avi Papatheodorou
Kiriakatis

167

Lou Pantages in front of the Paramount Theatre, ca. 1940s.
Courtesy of the Adams and Pantages Families

Walking down the street just before reaching High Street was the Court Theater, where we went to see movies on Saturday. The ticket for us was 11 cents, if you were shorter than the mark of the ticket window, but if you were taller, then you were charged 19 cents. We always approached the ticket window stooped over so that we could get in for 11 cents. For 11 cents you were presented a lot of show. This show consisted of three main films, a special feature film, the Saturday serial, and five cartoons; we didn't leave the movie house until about 6 p.m. We also sometimes had a cheaper way of getting in the theater by having someone open an emergency door and before the ushers could prevent illegal entrance, three or four of us would sneak in.

REVEREND GEORGE A. XENOFANES

My parents lived in the four-family house on Lindsey Street owned by Father Spyridakis, who also lived there. Our family was close friends of Father Spyridakis's family, spending Thanksgiving and Christmas with them every year. Every Thursday night my mother, Mrs. Spyridakis, Father Spyridakis, my father, and Gus Kitsos played bridge. On Tuesday nights my father would go to Dr. Antonius's or Mr. Adams's home to play cards.
Corrine Pappas Maskaleris

High Street was the location of many distinctive homes belonging to doctors practicing at the High Street location of St. Barnabas, and teachers and professors of the surrounding schools and colleges. Greek families living there were good, gracious people with an aristocracy having nothing to do with wealth. My mom and dad ran a grocery store with Greek products immediately next to St. Nick's, which, of course, thrust us into the center of Greek life.
Tess Demos Nomos

Newark was a great city to grow up in. The buses in town took you anywhere you wanted to go. The shopping was excellent. Hahne's was a favorite, as were L. Bamberger and Company, Orbach's, and Kresge department stores. Whenever we wanted to go out to play, we found friends outdoors. We played "kick the can," "ring a lario," roller-skated, and countless other games and activities. There were no play dates. On summer afternoons gathering in beautiful Branch Brook Park and rolling down the grassy hill to see who could reach the bottom first was great fun.
Ann Nikitakis Soppas

From left, friends Charles Coniaris, Charles Kostakos, and John Koronakos are in the back yard of their apartment, ca. 1930s.
Courtesy of Charles Kostakos

Our neighborhood around New Street (now the front door of Rutgers) was mostly Irish and German with a sprinkling of Blacks, a few Italians, and one family of WASPs (my best friend, Edward). I had Greek friends from church and cousins.
◦⁓ Spiro Poulos

We went to every Greek dance they had. That's how I met my wife.
◦⁓ Michael Paskas

As teenagers, we would go to the Greek dances, which were held almost every weekend. Since we lived so close to the downtown area (Nelson Place), we would walk to the movies and also to shop. We had a neighborhood movie theater called the Court Theater, which we went to almost every Saturday and Sunday. Tuesday night was amateur night, and Wednesday night was dish night. Every Greek home had the same dishes from the Court Theater.
◦⁓ Antoinette Markos Genakos

Greek dances were big events in our lives. I had two attractive sisters and a handsome brother. I remember [my sisters] dressing up, [with] upsweeps (hairdos), and going to see Tommy Dorsey and Greek bands at the Mosque Terrace. I was too young to go.
◦⁓ John Lollos

Standing from left on Napoleon Street, "Down Neck" Newark, are Nicholas Theodos, Keith Nicholas, Carol Theodos held by Helen Theodos, William Nicholas, a friend, and Anthony Nicholas, with Gus Theodos standing in front of the group, ca. 1930s.
Courtesy of Gus Theodos

Top to bottom, friends George Petine, Mike Paskas, and Bill Zervakos clown around on Summit Street, ca. 1943.
Courtesy of William Zervakos

My father, Gus, had many diverse interests. He studied the English language and translated medical instructions gratis for Greek patients of Dr. Kessler at the Kessler Institute.
CORINNE PAPPAS MASKALERIS

169

Evelyn, Spiro, and Artemis Vardakis are
enjoying a Sunday in Military Park, ca. 1943.
Courtesy of Artemis Vardakis

The Greek American community joins in the
celebration of Newark's three hundredth
anniversary parade, 1966.
*Courtesy of St. Nicholas Greek Orthodox
Church, Newark*

We used to sneak in to the Court Theater on Nelson Place. One of us would pay the 10-cent admission, then open the window in the men's room to let the others in.
— William Chirgotis

The first museum that I visited with my folks was the Newark Museum, and I remember also leisurely strolls through Branch Brook Park when the cherry blossoms were in bloom and Father rowing us across the lake. Shopping with Evelyn in downtown Newark at Bamberger's, Kresge's, or Hahne's, stopping at Schraft's for a bite to eat, and after that maybe taking in a movie at Loews, Adams, Paramount, or Branford.
— Artemis Vardakis

The Thanksgiving Day parade came down West Market Street and ended at Bamberger's at Washington Street. Anyone who had a home on West Market Street was very popular, and the kids would fill the fire escapes to view the parade.
— Kostas Diamandas

In 1914 we attended a World War I bond rally in Military Park. Mary Pickford was on stage. I was six or seven years old.
— Joanna Gellas

Steve Maskaleris served in the Army Air Corps during World War II as a member of the Army Air Force Band, known as the Glenn Miller Band. The band played every Sunday on the radio and marched in parades, even after Glenn Miller was reported missing in action.
— Corrine Pappas Maskaleris

Newark's Americans of Greek descent continue their personal odysseys throughout the United States. Although the ethnic enclave is no longer identified with a specific neighborhood, the Greek community still exists through friends, relatives, *koumbari*, churches, and businesses. Through active participation in the communities where they live and work, they continue to enhance the legacy of their parents, grandparents, great-grandparents, and relatives. Having become one of the most successful ethnic groups in the country, the talent, energy, and spirit of the American Greeks have combined the best ideals of their culture and traditions from two worlds—the United States and Greece.

Chris and Mary Vasilow are Christmas shopping on Broad Street in December 1949.
Courtesy of Mary Gianas Vasilow

Mr. and Mrs. Halulakos enjoy a quiet moment sitting by the statue of Lincoln in front of the courthouse on the corner of Springfield Avenue and West Market Street, ca. 1940s.
Courtesy of Norma Poulakos

We had permanent taxi service because we did not have a car. We had ice delivered to our home, by the pound, because there was no refrigeration. We had a wagon that frequently came to sharpen my mother's knives, [and] homeless people who knocked on my parents' door were always fed by my mother. We went to the movies every Saturday after we completed our household chores.
EFFIE MASKALERIS VLAHAKES

Celebrating Constantine Stathopoulos' name day on the roof 51 West Market Street are the Stathopoulos family, from left: Sarantos with Diana in front of him and Vassiliki holding Constantine. With them are friends Fotini and Vageli Poulos with their children. May 21, 1920.
Courtesy of Diana Stathopoulos

I recall how my father loved life and especially how he loved to dance. He danced the intricate folk dances of his village with such delicate grace and agility that the strength and power of his stock frame were belied. On Saturday nights, he would invite musicians and compatriots to our home. They would spend the night dancing. We watched sleepily with wide-eyed innocence as these men nostalgically danced. My father led the circle of men; they swayed in rhythm while he pivoted, knelt on his haunches, leapt into the air, then daintily twirled, all in time to the folk music.

ANASTASIA G. BRAVAKIS FOR THEODORE JOHN BRAVAKIS

Tess Demas is enjoying the sunshine on her face as she sits on a rooftop above Washington Street, ca. 1950s.
Courtesy of Tess Demas Nomos

The years we lived through as youngsters will seem quite alien to our youth of today who have cell phones, computers, cars, and don't mind spending $3 for a fashionable cup of coffee . . . . Here is some perspective on our early years in Newark, but bear in mind salaries were rock bottom as well: In the mid-1930s one could buy a new car for $500 and possibly less, a gallon of gasoline was 10 cents . . . sugar was a nickel a pound, bread was 8 cents a loaf, a postage stamp was 3 cents . . . bananas were 10 cents a dozen and you could pick your own off a huge bunch that hung on a hook . . . . There was little or no television, so we read books, listened to the radio, and played games . . . . The most daring things we did in school were throw around blackboard erasers and shoot spitballs . . . . I didn't see nylons until the 1939 World's Fair in New York . . . . There was no nudity, sex, or foul language in movies . . . . There was no Garden State Parkway, and cars weren't air conditioned, so the ride to the shore was long and hot . . . . That's what it was like in the early-to mid-twentieth century. We were pulled out of the Great Depression by the Second World War, which brought us Rosie the Riveter and women doing much of men's work while brothers and sons went to war . . . . More than forty years later, I remember with fondness the innocent times that we lived in, as well as a gentility that now seems to belong to the past. Our parents became American citizens because they wanted to, and our own citizenship is a benefit of that act. My hope is that their descendants will never forget their roots, or the extraordinary challenges encountered and dealt with by those early Greek immigrants who crossed an ocean in search of a better life.

HELEN GALANOPLOS

In front of 61 Nelson Place are Peter Pallantios, Gus Stathopoulos, and James Pallantios, ca. 1943.
Courtesy of James Pallantios

Below: John Koronakos, in Navy uniform, is with his cousin, Maria Gianakouris, and his brother, Chris, ca. 1944.
Courtesy of John Koronakos

Father automatically became a citizen in 1917, as did Mother because he was a U.S. World War I vet.
CALLIOPE DADENAS GEANNAKAKES

Street Scenes

Kiki and Demi Lampros, standing in front of their father's store on Springfield Avenue, are ready for church, ca. 1940s.
Courtesy of the Lampros Family

Garifala and Kalliope Kapandais are on their way to school, ca. 1937.
Courtesy of Garifalia Kapandais Mellas

I worked at the Prudential for eight years and walked from Washington Street to the Roseville area with Ann Nikitakis Soppas many times without fear.
BESSIE KOSTINS MAMALOU

George Petine, with a friend, stands in Military Park with Broad Street behind them, ca. 1950s.
Courtesy of Pannoria Petine

Sophie Kapandais stands on the courthouse steps on April 20, 1941.
Courtesy of Garifalia Kapandais Mellas

There were horse-drawn wagons from which we could buy fresh produce in season and large cubes of ice in varying sizes for our iceboxes, the largest at 50 cents. The ice would slowly melt and drip into a pan that was placed under the icebox. An old Jewish man would traverse the neighborhood in his wagon calling for "Rags! Rags!" Dugan's delivered bread; all one had to do was put the placard with a big D on it in the window. The milkman delivered butter, eggs, and milk in bottles with three inches of cream at the top; in winter, the cream would freeze and pop the cap. That frozen cream was ambrosia! I can still hear the rattle of empty milk bottles being picked up in the early hours of the morning.

HELEN GALANOPLOS

Andrew Dokas is playing softball on the street at Nelson Place,
ca. 1950s.
Courtesy of Nicholas Linardakis

In the apartment house there ware all Greek women . . . our baby carriages were downstairs. Together we
would go shopping with our baby carriages. One would help the other because we didn't have automobiles.
We would go to the Greek grocer, Mr. Pallantios (Bertha's father), to Academy Street, Springfield Avenue,
and Prince Street. We filled the carriages because we also had children—I had two walking and one in
the carriage . . . . Socially we associated with Greeks, but the children had school friends . . . diverse
neighborhood . . . visited on Sundays . . . children played softball on Stirling Street (twenty-five to thirty
kids), on other Sundays (springtime), we had picnics at Branch Brook Park after church.
JENNIE MOUTIS

Connie and Louis Geannakakes are outside their home in their Roseville neighborhood, ca. 1940s
Courtesy of the Vlahakes Family

Peter and Toni Markos are with their cousin, Tommy Markos, on Nelson Place, ca. 1940s.
Courtesy of the Sam Markos Family

My brother, George, started working for B&B Press and Peter Bistis as an errand boy delivering menus to restaurants. He was a ladies man who wanted to look good to impress the waitresses. Wanting to look like Valentino, he plastered his hair with sugar and water. The only thing he attracted was flies.

THEODORE J. BRAVAKIS

Endnotes

1. "Knowing Newark." *The Star-Ledger*, April 19, 2001, Charles F. Cummings.

2. *The Greeks: A Great Adventure*. Isaac Asimov. 1965, pp. 298–99.

3. "The New Jersey Ethnic Experience." B. Cunningham, ed., 1977, essay by Chrysanthy Kehayes Greico.

4. GOARCH.org. Web page for Greek Orthodox Archdiocese of America

5. 1957 history of St. Nicholas written for an ad journal.

6. Published notice to the parishioners of the Greek Orthodox Church of the community of Newark, New Jersey (including: invitation to general assembly published 2/7/1917, letter from parish priest to community dated 2/14/1917). Courtesy of Calomira Papageorgiou Canaris and translated by Vasiliki Diamandas.

7. "Knowing Newark." *The Star-Ledger*, April 19, 2001, Charles F. Cummings.

8. AHEPA.org. Web page of American Hellenic Educational Progressive Association (AHEPA), 73.

Appendices

St. Nicholas Parish Council Presidents

Peter Penek	1904
George Panagos	1908
John Semetis	1913
Argyris P. Argyris	1922–1934
Adam A. Adams	1935–1938
Demosthenis Gevas	1939–1940
Milton Matheakis	1941–1942
Nicholas Saros	1943
John C. Demos	1944
Michael J. Pappas	1945–1946
Thomas A. Argyris	1947–1948
James T. Gellas	1949–1950
William G. Chirgotis	1951–1957
Peter T. Zafferes	1958–1960
George Maroulakos	1961–1972
Spyros Dendrinos	1973–1975
Roy D. Soppas	1976–1979
Nick G. Paras	1980–1982
John Tsaptsinos	1983–1986
Spero Margeotes	1987–1991
Paul G. Jemas	1992–1994
Gus Theodos	1995–Present

St. Demetrios Parish Council Presidents

Demetrios Chrisoveris	1930s and 1940s
Costas Moskoyiannis	
Michael Hatzimihalis	
Odysseas Neres	
Costas Mumtzis	
George Agalias	
Peter Thomas	
Peter Thomas	1950s, 1960s, and 1970s
Gus Makris	
Peter Kokkalis	
Gus Stravelakis	
Andrew Agriantonis	
Gus Genakos	
Gus Stravelakis	

Anastasios Soros

Elias Loucopoulos   1980s (move to Union 1984)

St. Nicholas Greek Orthodox Church Historic Events

1901   Lyric Hall, 303 Plane Street (now University Avenue)
1913   149 Academy Street
1924   555 High Street (now Martin Luther King, Jr. Boulevard)

On July 11, 1906, at a general meeting at Lyric Hall, Number 303 Plane Street, in the City of Newark, their usual place of meeting for public worship, the following trustees were elected to incorporate St. Nicholas Greek Orthodox Church of Newark in the State of New Jersey, the County of Essex. They included:

George Pappas

Nicholas Pulos

George Kanelles

Haridimos Papa Haridimou

Manuel Joannides

According to the 1908 church ledger, on January 17, 1908, the St. Nicholas community elected the following officers to assume the responsibilities of the church with authorization to spend $5,000 to buy property to build the church:

President	*George Panagos*
Secretary	*Nicholas Assimacopoulos*
Treasurer	*F. N. Karatzas*
Members:	*Michael Angelopoulos*
	Alex Platis
	Demetrios Panopalis
	Theodore Demopoulos
	Keriacos Henos
	Panagiotis Panagos

On November 28, 1909, the guarantors of the mortgage were:

K. G. Pappas

Panagiotis Panagos

Christos Brousalis

George Bacos

Christos Panagos

Nicholas Tsoutsalas

George Panagos

The 1913 church ledger donated by George Tzavalas (Gavalas) stated that on December 28, 1913, Reverend Thomas Papageorgiou, the parish priest, President John Semetis, Secretary P. N. Rusopoulos, Treasurer Constantine A. Psychogios, and Councilman Basil G. Vathis decided to pay off the mortgage balance of $1,800.

Major donors included:

$150 each

George Tzavalas (Gavalas)

George Bacos

Constantine Pappas

Polycarpos Papastavrou

$50

Reverend Thomas Papageorgiou

$25 each

Constantine Psychogios

The Brothers Kalanari

Donations from residents of Newark and surrounding communities:

$240	88 residents of Newark
$28	13 residents of Dover
$26	11 residents of Elizabeth
$25	10 residents of Jersey City
$16	15 residents of Montclair
$18	8 residents of Morristown
$25	10 residents of New Brunswick
$27	10 residents of Passaic
$71	22 residents of Paterson
$18.50	8 residents of Perth Amboy
$29	20 residents of Plainfield
$40.50	15 residents of Trenton
$53.75	18 residents of Harrisburg, PA

Temporary parish council of 1917:

George Penek

Panagiotis Psychogios

Themistocles Nickolopoulos

Basil Vathis

Nikolaos Theodorou

Demetrios Vasiliki

1918 Board of Trustees:
Adam A. Adams
Argyris Argyris
George Gavalas (Tzavalas)
Gus Kitsos
William Maskaleris
Gus Pappas
E. N. Plates
Gus Speros

1924 Building Committee:
Adam A. Adams
E. N. Plates
Argyris Argyris
William Maskaleris
Gus Pappas

Restaurants, Luncheonettes, and Candy Shops

Courtesy of Peter Markos

1. Academy Luncheonette
2. Apollo Diner—Demetroulakos and Thomas
3. Arvanites Luncheon & Soda Fountain—Arvanites Family
4. Atlantic Coffee Pot Luncheonette—Christos Family
5. Boston Candy Company—Nicholas Lampros
6. Branford Restaurant—James Lanaris
7. Broad Restaurant
8. Brothers Restaurant—James and Gus Gellas
9. C&D Luncheonette—George Visas
10. Candy stand by Loews Theater—Tom Gellas
11. Candy store—James Billias
12. Candy store and soda fountain—George Pontiakos
13. Capital Restaurant—Peter Jovanis
14. Central Coffee Pot—George Petropoulos
15. Central Restaurant—Bill Amprazis and Vagelis Parmakis
16. Central Restaurant—Matthews Family
17. Chris's Sweet Shoppe—Chris Sarandoulias
18. Confectionery and Soda Fountain Store—Chris Vasiliow
19. Court Luncheonette
20. Court Restaurant—Boucouvalas Family
21. Crystal Candy Shoppe—P. Georges

22. Crystal Coffee Shop—Vasilios and Andreas Koukousis
23. Dino's Restaurant—Gus Genakos
24. Essex Restaurant—Gus and Angelo Gevas
25. Famous Restaurant—Zervis and Kacades
26. Fisher Luncheonette—Foltis Family
27. George's Coffee Shop—Spiros Vlahos, George Papasavas, and Steve Tseppes
28. George's Restaurant—George Kapetanos
29. Gevas Restaurant—Gus and Angelo Gevas
30. Goody Sweet shop—Angelo Sarantos
31. Gus's Luncheonette—Gus Kostas
32. Hall Restaurant—Demetroulakos and Thomas
33. Hugo's Luncheonette—George Mendrinos
34. John Pogidas Restaurant—Pogidas Family
35. John's Luncheonette—John Nikitakis
36. L&M Luncheonette—Sam Markos
37. Little Presto—Aridas Family
38. Malamis Luncheonette—Peter Malamis
39. New Adelphia Restaurant—Sam Markos
40. New Dana Coffee Shop—Amprazis and Parmakis
41. New Sinclair Deli & Restaurant—Nick and George
42. Oasis Restaurant—Ted Reid
43. P&A Luncheonette—Theophilos and Kallianis
44. Parker's Restaurant—Steve Aprazis
45. Post Grill Diner—Skouras Family
46. Presto Restaurant—Gavalas and Maskaleris
47. Prudential Luncheonette—Theophilos Brothers
48. Renaissance Restaurant—Ted Reid
49. Rialto Restaurant—DeNicholas Family
50. Royal Restaurant—Mike and Nick Mastakas
51. Scotty's diners—Mavrades, Mesenazos, Harris
52. Scouras Lunchroom—Scouras Family
53. Skyway Restaurant—James Gonis and Jerry Agalias
54. Sofia Restaurant—Gus Gondevas and Angelo Delapotas
55. South Park Restaurant—Moutis Family
56. Star Central Restaurant
57. Steve's Sandwich Shop—Kefalas Family
58. Terzis Confectionery & Luncheonette—Tony Drivas and Costas Vasilakos
59. Thomas Restaurant—Thomas Family
60. U.S. Restaurant—Charles Hatzaras

61. United Sweet Shop—Steve Gevas and Brothers

62. United Tea Room—Gevas Brothers

63. Vranas Candy Store—Vranas Family

64. Washington Restaurant—James Lanaris

65. Wonder Restaurant—Jimmy Demetropoulos

Florists / Floral Companies

1. Arcadia Florist—Bill Zervakos

2. Branford Florist—Pappaliou Brothers

3. Exotic Florist—Harry Staikos

4. Forest Hill Floral Company Inc.—Louis Zois and William Zois

5. Lollos Florist—George Lollos

6. New Jersey Evergreen Company—Mavrodi and Poulos

7. Penek Florist—William Penek

8. Roseland Florist—Arthur Staikos

9. Washington Florist—Zois Brothers

Barbers and Shoe Parlors

1. George's Barber Shop—George Vasiliou

2. Shoe Shine Parlor—George Argyris

3. Staikos Barber Shop—John Staikos

Tailors, Hat Cleaners, and Clothing Shops

1. Tailor Shop—Gus

2. Tailor Shop—John Vasiliades

3. Tailor Shop—Spyridon Basil Kehayes

4. Hat Cleaner—Jim

5. Hat cleaner—Soterios Coniaris

6. Furrier—John Eugene

7. Paris Fur Shop

8. Argyris Shoppe: Lingerie, Hosiery and Sportswear—Esther Argyris

Ice Distributor

1. Ice Distributor—John Bravakis

Baking Companies

1. Holsum Bread Company—Anthony Javas and Brothers

2. Lemnos Baking Company—Chletsos Family

3. Olympia Bread Company—Pyriles Family

Coffeehouses and Bars

1. To Kronion Coffeehouse—Alex and Harry

2. Coffeehouse—Barba Andrea

3. Coffeehouse—Barba Stathis

4. Coffeehouse—Barba Iannis

5. Coffeehouse—Koutsoubelis Family

6. Pool hall and bar—Gus Pappas

7. Dreamland Bar & Grill—John Jolas

8. Boulevard Bar & Grill—Kostas Sampatakos and Louis Geracos

Coffee Companies

1. Aroma Coffee Company—Faraklas Brothers

2. Java Coffee Company—Yeannakis Family

3. N. Juvelis Coffee Company—Juvelis Family

Delicatessens, Grocery, and Specialty Stores

1. Alevras Deli—Alevras Family

2. Atlas Wholesale Food Distributors—Bill Gougoumis

3. Demas Deli & Grocery—Demas Family

4. Efstathiou Brothers Food Market—Efstathiou Family

5. Greek Products & Newspapers—Dermousis Family

6. Greek Store—Papastamatis Family

7. Janulis Delicatessen—T. Janulis

8. Karis Paper & Food Distributors—Karis Family

9. Kounelias Deli—Kounelias Family

10. Liberty Food Market—Diamandas Family

11. O.K. Fish Market—Apolon Buclary

12. Paramount Food Market—Tom and Bertha Manos

13. Petine Brothers Deli—Nick, Jim, George, and Dick

14. Potami Grocery—Kapandais Family

15. Soumas Grocery and Butcher Shop—Soumalakakis Family

16. Tsairis Groceries—Tsairis Cousins

17. Warren Fruit Market—William Mehalaris

Print Shops, Machine Shops, Auto Repair Shops, and Suppliers

1. B&B Press—Bistis Brothers

2. E. N. Plates Stationery—E. N. Plates

3. Godfriend's Print Shop—Harry Godfriend

4. Merit Press—Theodore J. Bravakis

5. Popular Home Improvement — James Post

6. Angelo's Hugo Body Shop, Inc.—Angelo Kostakes

7. International Manufactory Screw Co.—Michael Gargas

8. Arrow Machine Shop—S. Chimenides

9. Federal Restaurant Supply—Pete Pappas

Theaters, Radio/Music Stores, and Photographers

1. Adams Theatre — Adam A. Adams
2. Paramount Theatre — Adam A. Adams
3. Broad & Market Radio and Music Stores — Steve Argyris
4. Kapetan Studios: Photographer — George Kapetanos

Doctors, Dentists, Lawyers, and Pharmacists

1. Dr. Nicholas Antonius, M.D.
2. Dr. John Coniaris, M.D.
3. Dr. Anthony Malavazos, M.D.
4. Dr. Peter Poulos, M.D.
5. Dr. Charles Critides, D.D.S.
6. Dr. Steven Aridas, D.O.
7. Dr. Charles Coniaris, O.D.
8. A. Papadopoulos—Pharmacist
9. Thomas A. Argyris—Attorney
10. J. Pappas & J. Apostolakos—Attorneys
11. Louis Pantages—Attorney
12. Saros & Thevos—Attorneys

Parish Priests

St. Nicholas Greek Orthodox Church

Reverend Adamakos	1901
Reverend Prousianos	1907–1909
Reverend Daskalakis	1910–1912
Reverend Thomas Papageorge	1912–1918
Reverend George Spyridakis	1918–1954
Reverend James A. Aloupis	1954–2001
Reverend R. Nicholas Rafael	2001–2003
Reverend Thomas Tsevas	2003
Reverend Alexander Leondis	2004–2005
Reverend Constantine Makrinos	2005–present

St. Demetrios Greek Orthodox Church

Reverend Nicholas Papademetriou (Pappas)	1928–1929
Reverend Nicholas Triandafilou	1930–1931
Reverend Nicholas Papademetriou	1932–1952
Reverend Christopher Condoleon	1952–1981
Reverend Constantine Xirouhakis	1981–1995 (move to Union 1984)

Index

Author and Exhibit Co-curator

Angelique Lampros

Angelique Lampros, a native of Newark, New Jersey, now residing in West Orange, is fortunate to have been born an American of Greek descent. Her Hellenic heritage, its culture, traditions, and her active participation in organizations promoting its ideals have enriched her life. Documenting the Greek experience in Newark was a natural outgrowth of her interest in the history of Greece and pride in her Hellenic ancestry. The outcome was a successful three-month exhibit at the Newark Public Library, of which she was co-curator.

An educator and administrator, she retired from the District of South Orange–Maplewood where she was active in professional organizations and was a co-author of two books for teachers and students. Angelique has a B.A. from Montclair State University and an M.A. from George Washington University.

Her travels and varied experiences continue to broaden and enhance her love of the arts and humanities.

Exhibit Co-curator

Peter Markos

Peter Markos, an American Greek whose parents migrated from Sparta, Greece, in the 1920s, was born, raised, and educated in the public schools of Newark, New Jersey. He attended Robert Treat Junior High School and graduated from West Side High School in 1954. Markos holds Masters in Student Personnel Services and School Administration.

His began his career in 1961 as a high school science teacher, later became a guidance counselor, and during the last fourteen years of his career was an administrator. He retired in 1997 after thirty-six years in the Roselle, New Jersey, school district.

On October 19, 2002, Peter co-curated an exhibition titled "Remembering Newark's Greeks: An American Odyssey" at the Newark Public Library that documented the history of the Greek community for the past one hundred years in Newark.

Presently, Peter continues to be an active member at Holy Trinity Greek Orthodox Church in Westfield, New Jersey, enjoys traveling with his wife, Elaine, and is a member of many educational and Greek organizations.

Peter Jovanis (forefront), Stelios Juvelis (leaning), and friends, ca. 1926.
Courtesy of the Juvelis Family

Mrs. Markos and Jim Pallantios admire his new car on Nelson Place, ca. 1950s.
Courtesy of the Sam Markos Family

Nor
their
Cou
Mas

Mrs. Coniaris with Venetia on West Market Street, 1923.
Courtesy of the Coniaris Family

The Kostas family, ca.1940s.
Courtesy of Angie Kostas Hamilton

Costa
Nicho